PANIC AND COCO PRESENTS:
HOW TO DRAW SHAPES

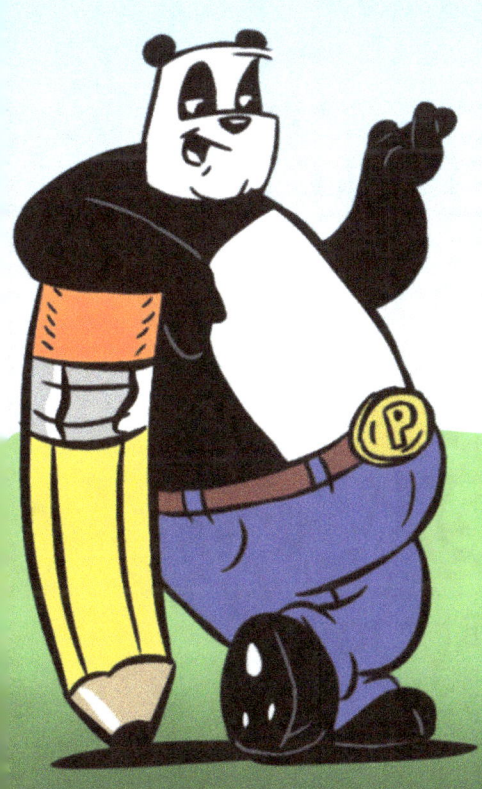
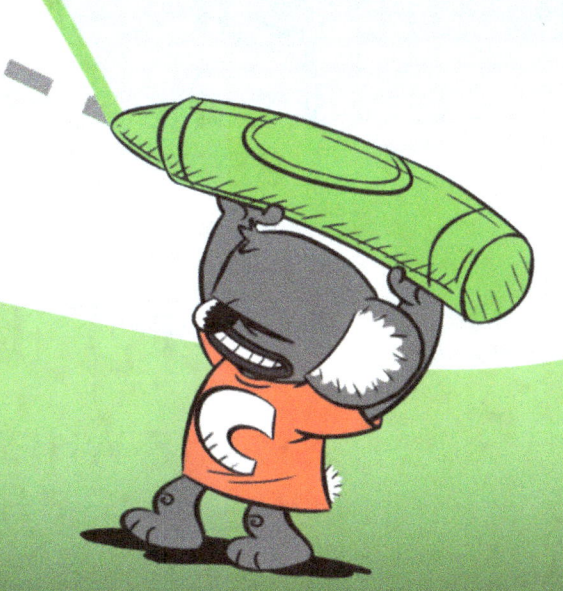

PANIC & COCO
PRESENTS

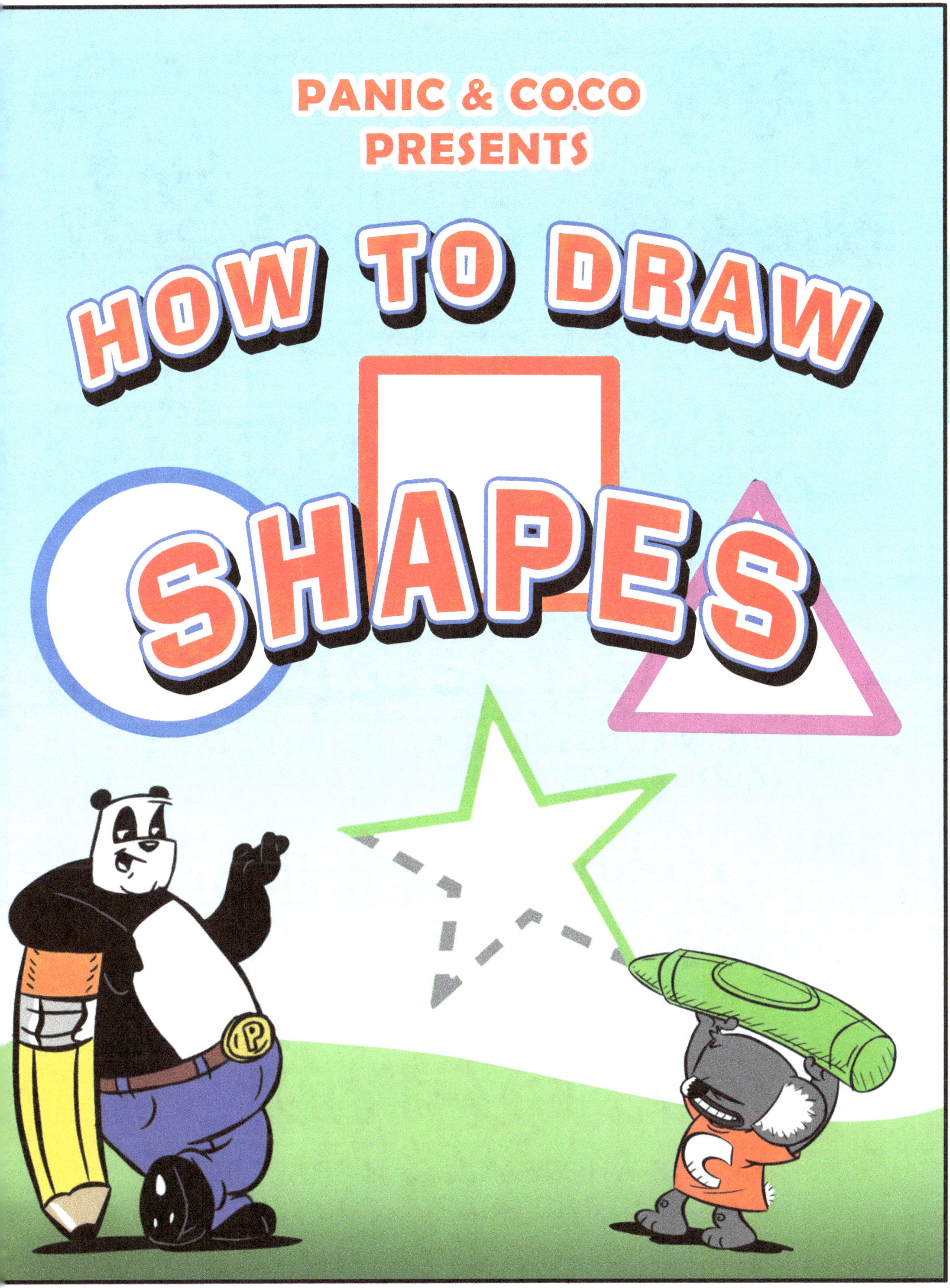

HOW TO DRAW

SHAPES

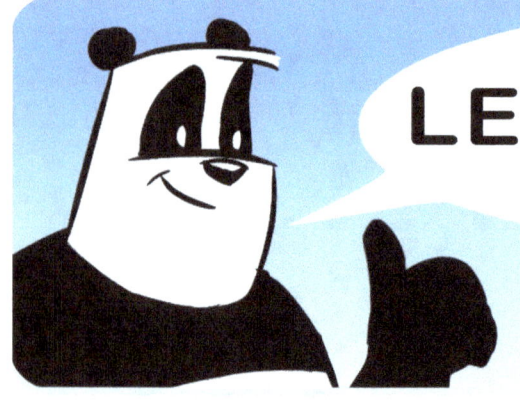 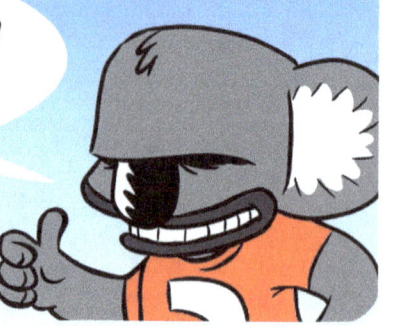

LET'S DRAW

HOW TO USE THIS BOOK

1 SHAPE EXAMPLES

YOU WILL SEE IMAGES OF OBJECTS WHICH HAVE THE NEXT SHAPE

2 SHAPE DESCRIPTION

WE WILL DESCRIBE GENERAL DETAILS ABOUT THE SHAPE

3 SHOWING YOU HOW

WE WILL SHOW YOU STEPS YOU CAN USE TO DRAW THE SHAPE

4 YOU TRY IT NOW

THIS IS WHERE YOU CAN PRACTICE DRAWING THE SHAPES YOURSELF

LEARN TO DRAW THESE FUN SHAPES

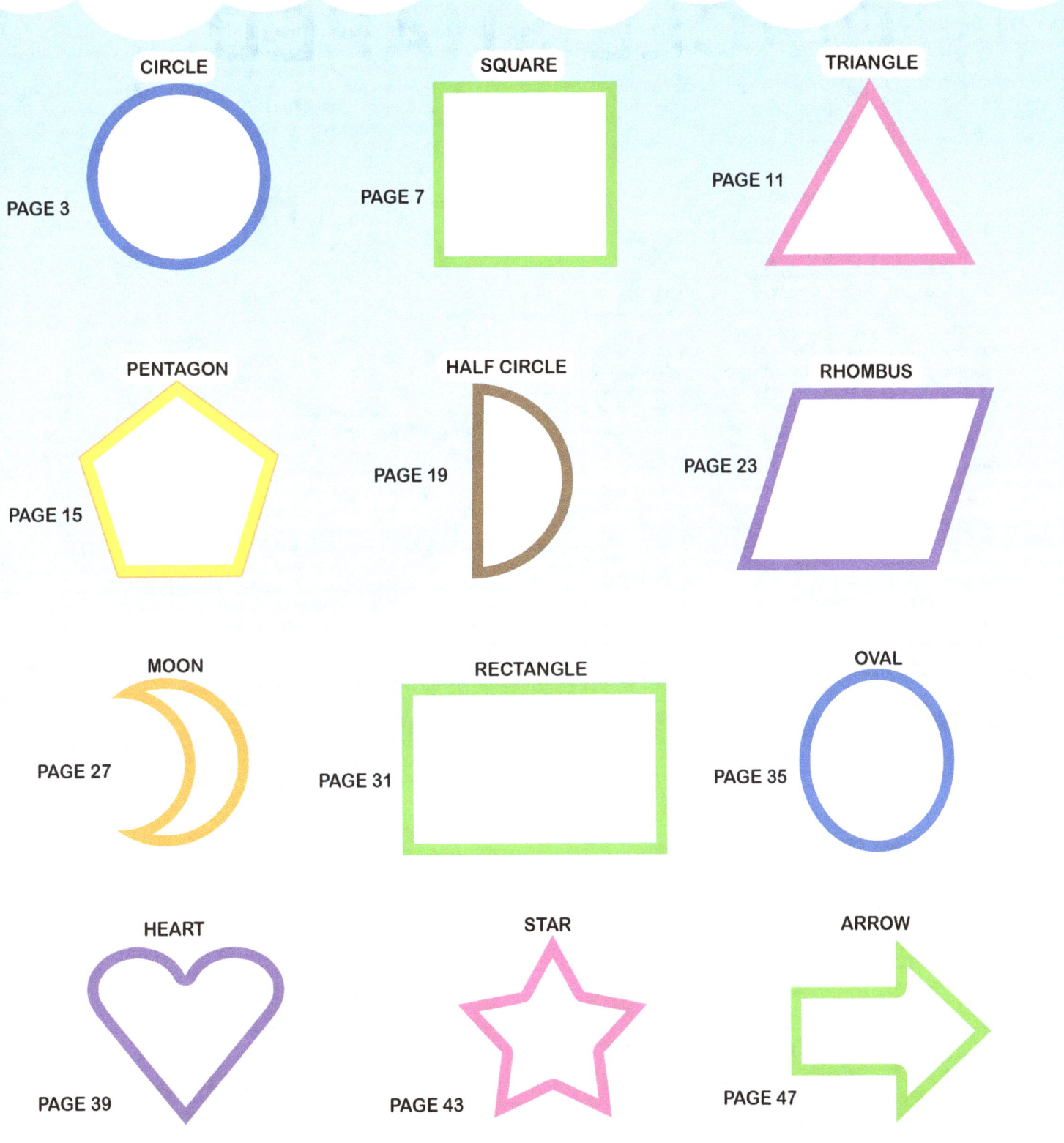

CIRCLE

PAGE 3

SQUARE

PAGE 7

TRIANGLE

PAGE 11

PENTAGON

PAGE 15

HALF CIRCLE

PAGE 19

RHOMBUS

PAGE 23

MOON

PAGE 27

RECTANGLE

PAGE 31

OVAL

PAGE 35

HEART

PAGE 39

STAR

PAGE 43

ARROW

PAGE 47

THESE OBJECTS ARE CIRCLE SHAPED:

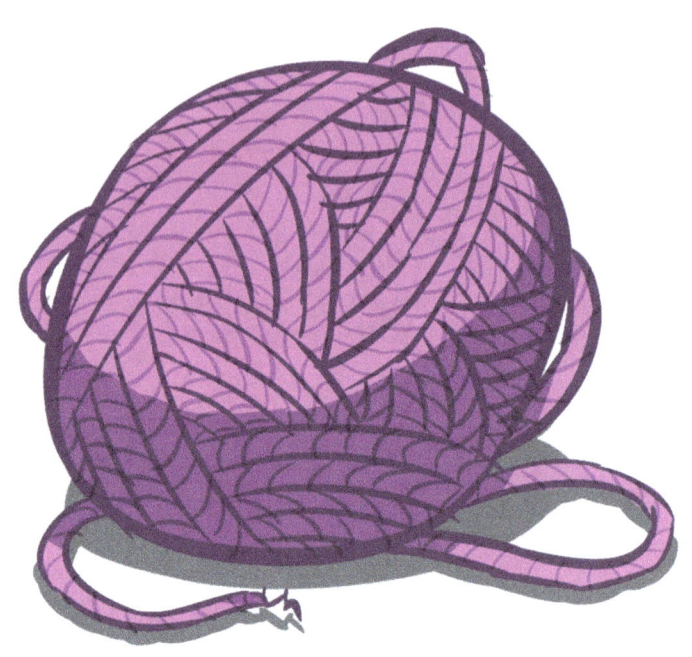
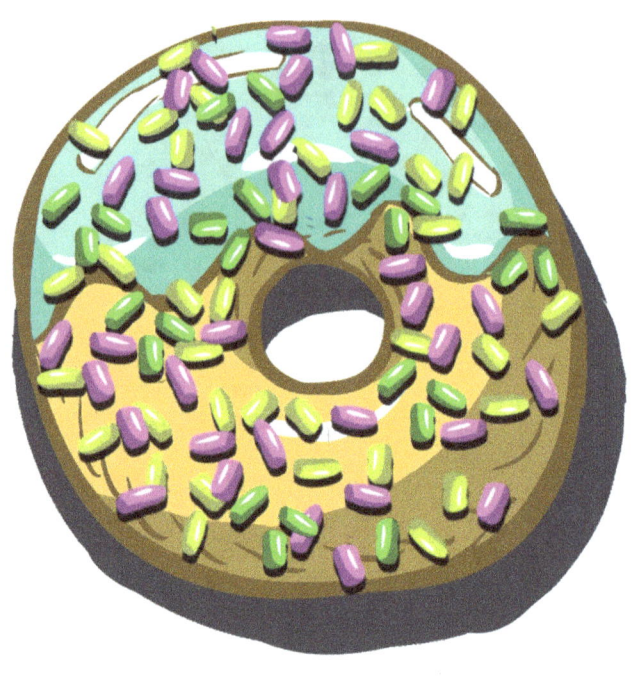
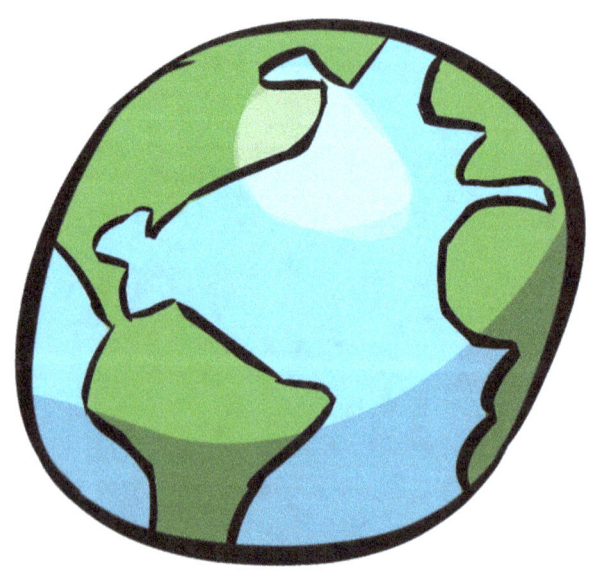
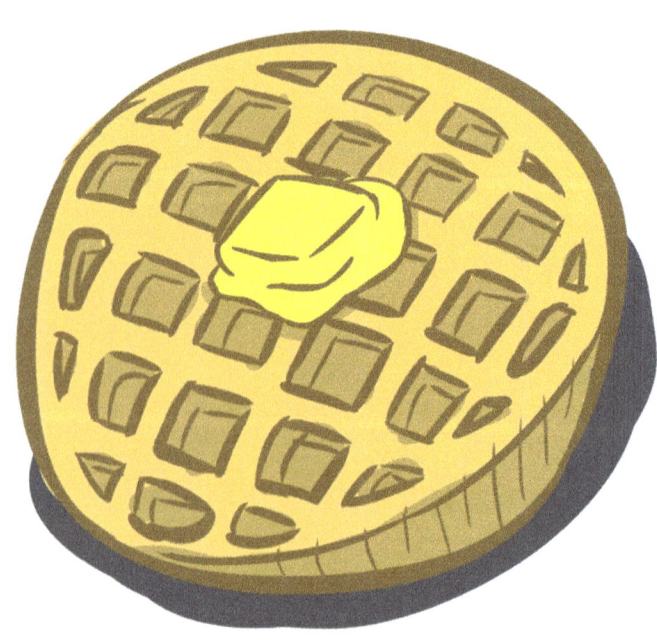

WHAT IS A CIRCLE ?

A ROUND SHAPE WITH NO CORNERS

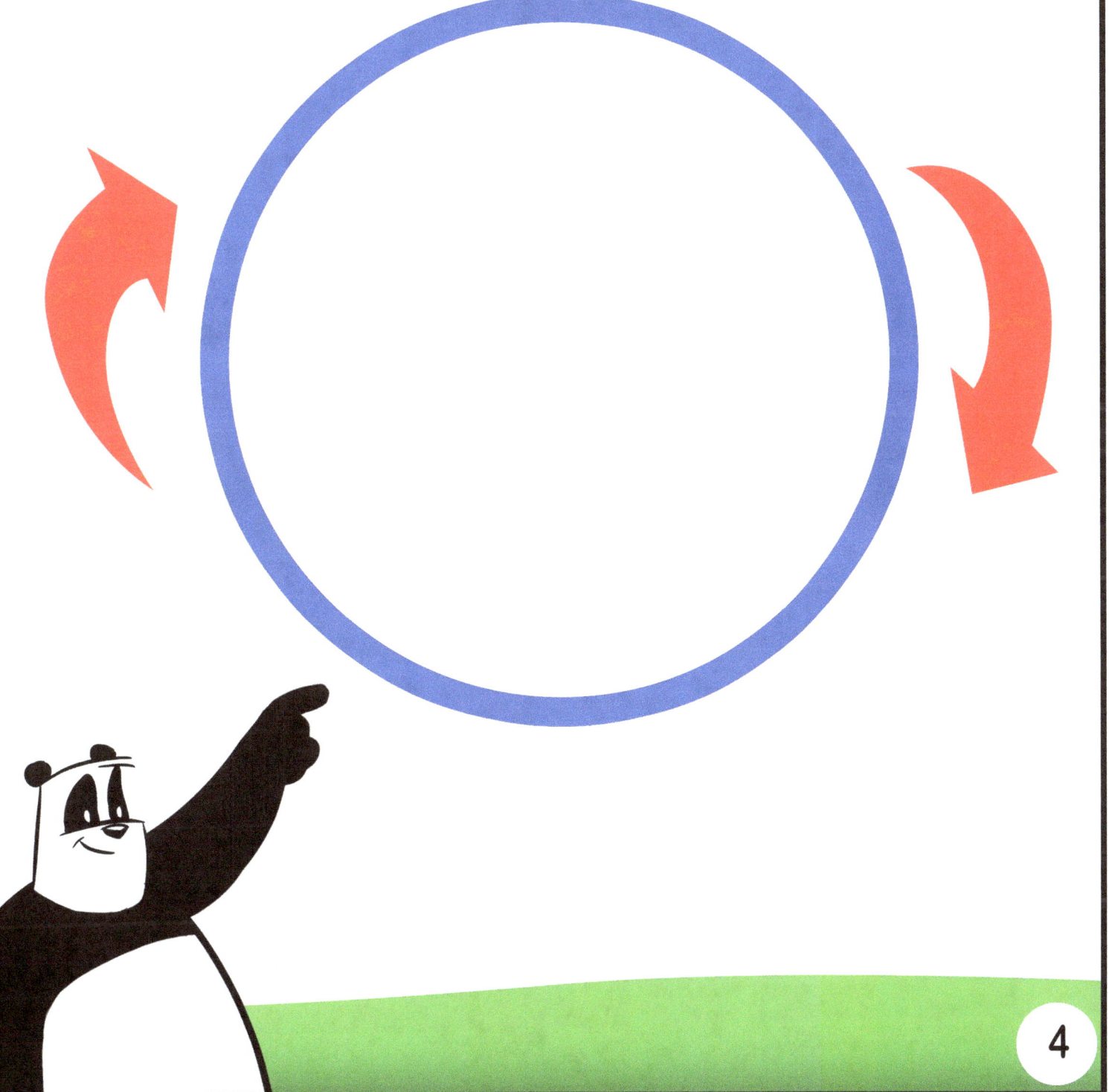

4

Follow these steps to draw this shape.

1

2

3

4

Now you can try to draw this shape.

Great job!
You did it!

THESE OBJECTS ARE SQUARE SHAPED:

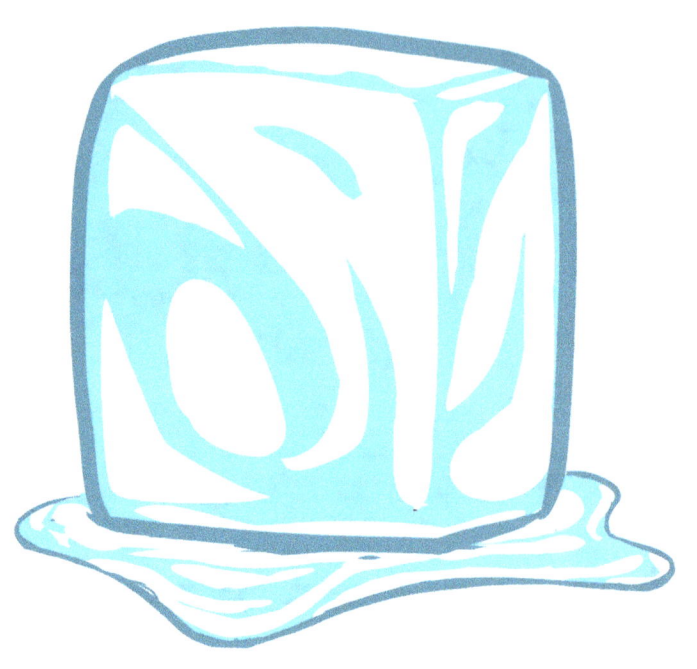
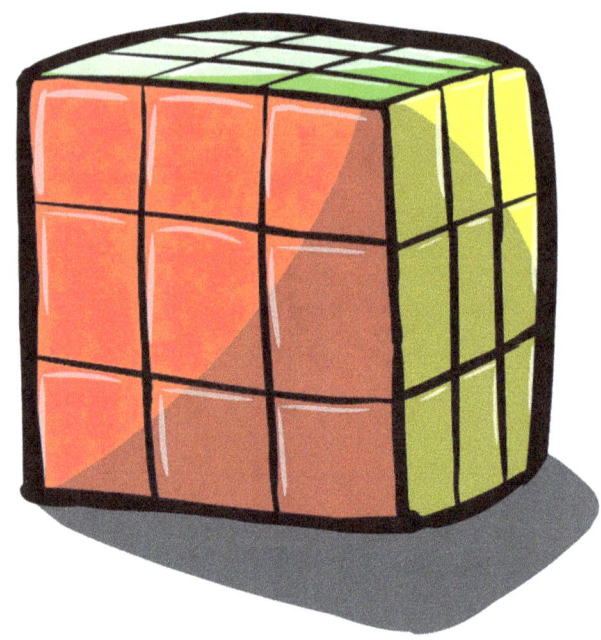

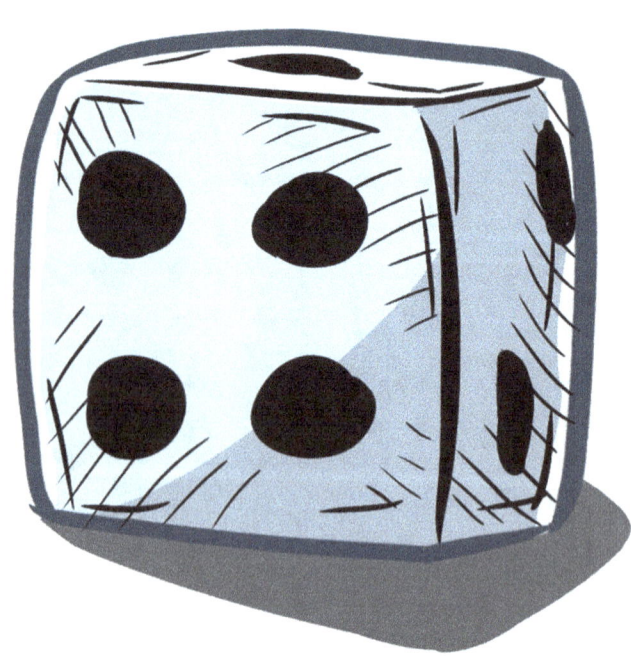

WHAT IS A SQUARE?

A SHAPE WITH FOUR STRAIGHT SIDES OF THE SAME LENGTH.

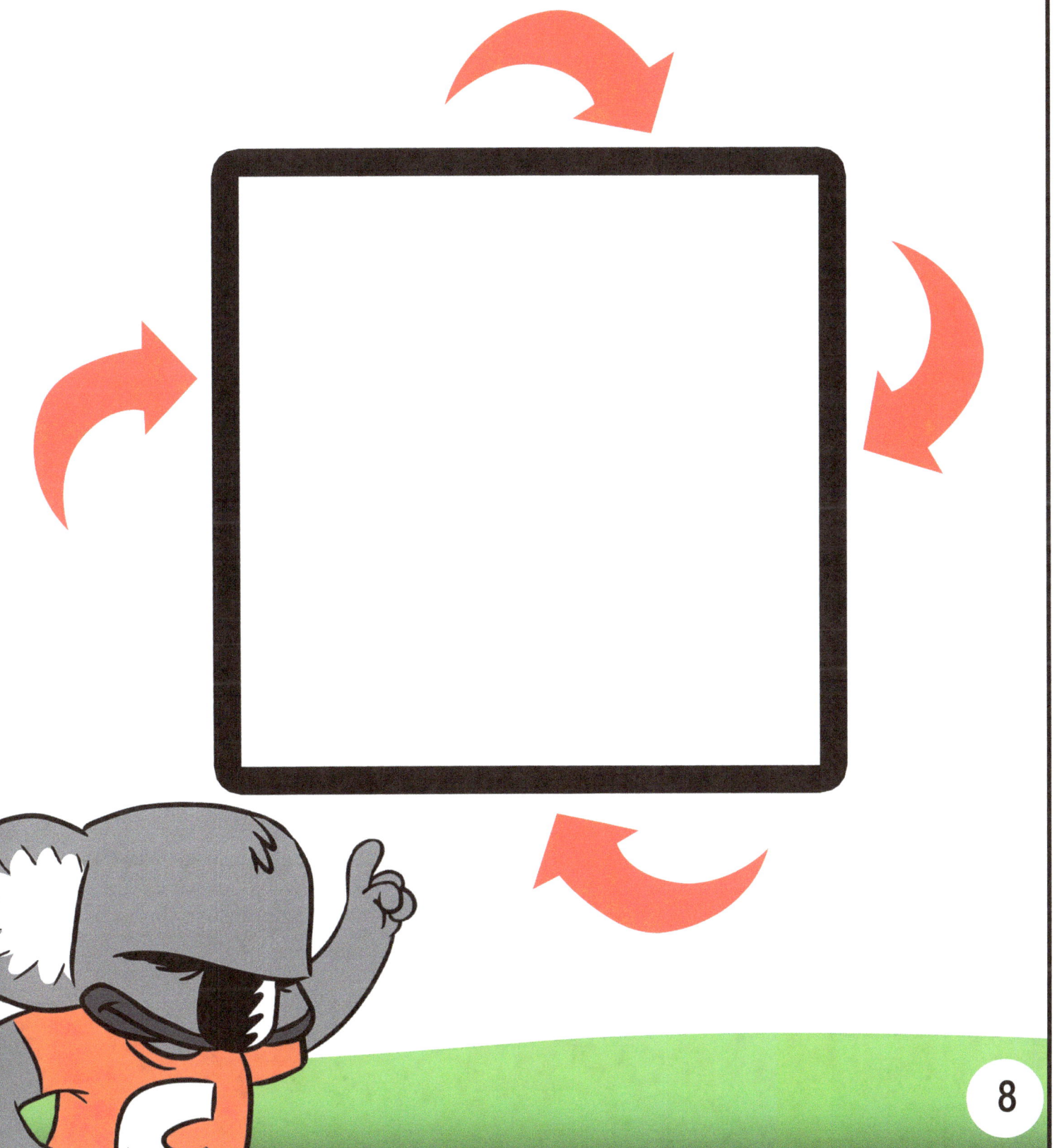

Follow these steps to draw this shape.

1

2

3

4

Now you can try to draw this shape.

That's Awesome!

10

THESE OBJECTS ARE TRIANGLE SHAPED:

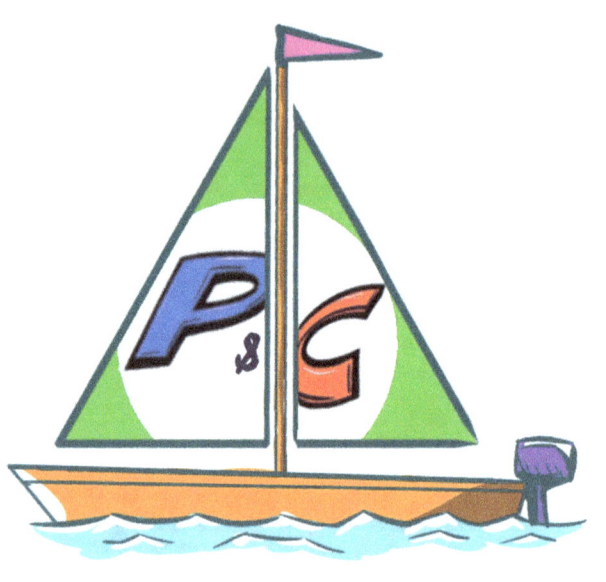

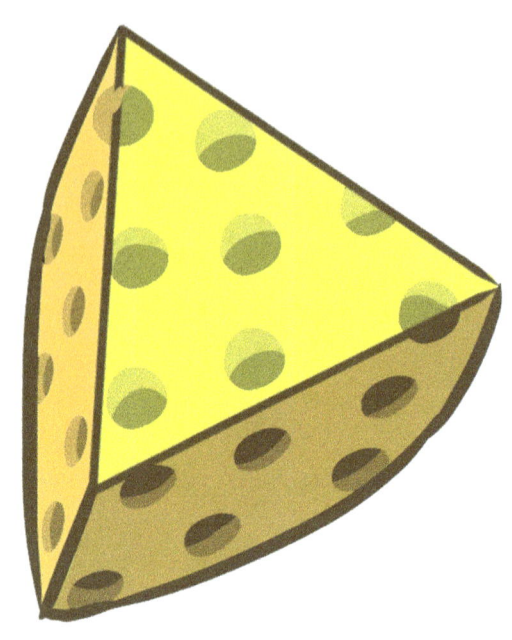

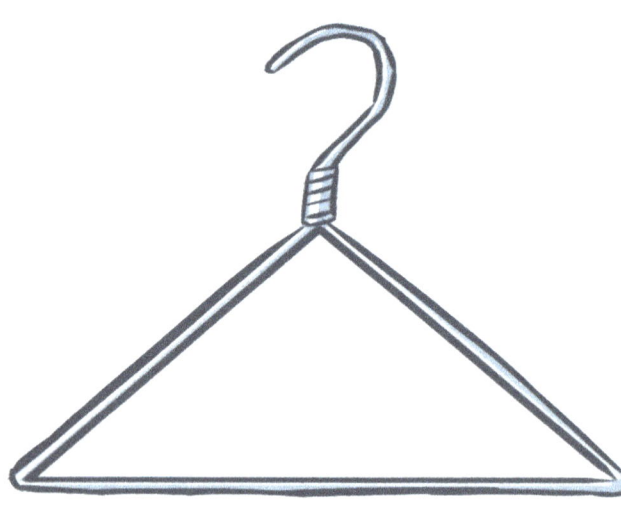

WHAT IS A TRIANGLE?

A SHAPE WITH THREE FLAT SIDES.

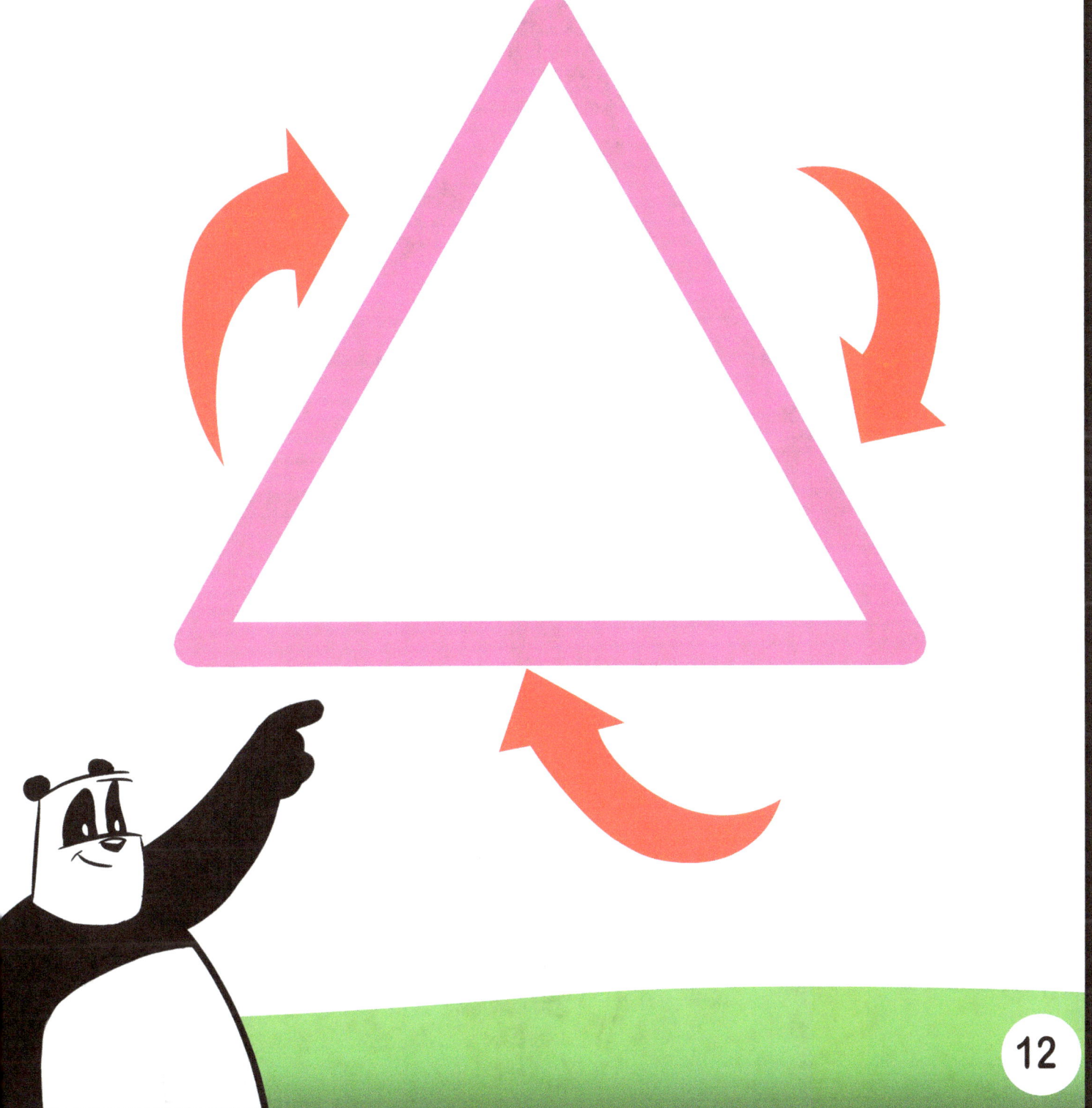

Follow these steps to draw this shape.

1

2

3

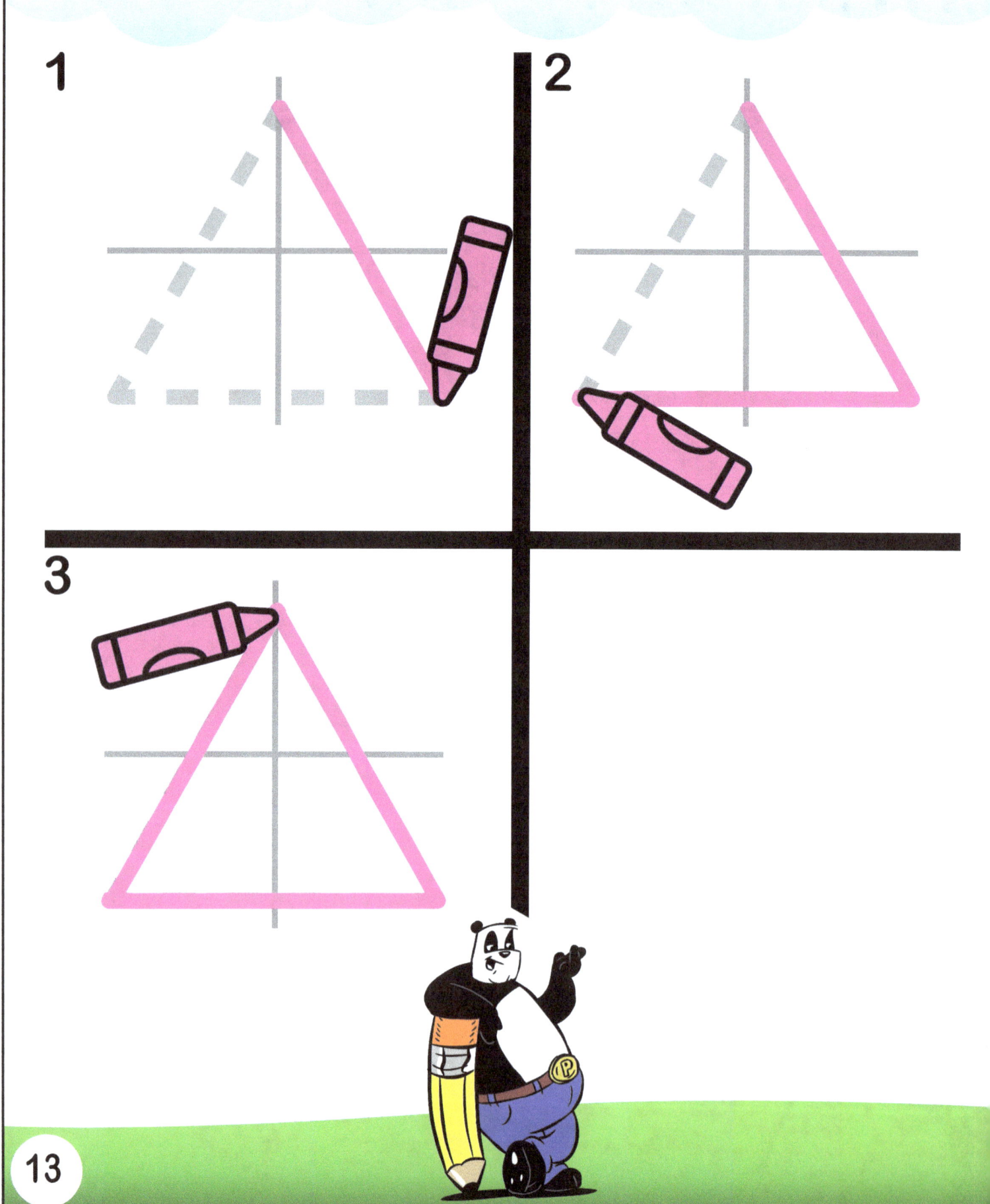

Now you can try to draw this shape.

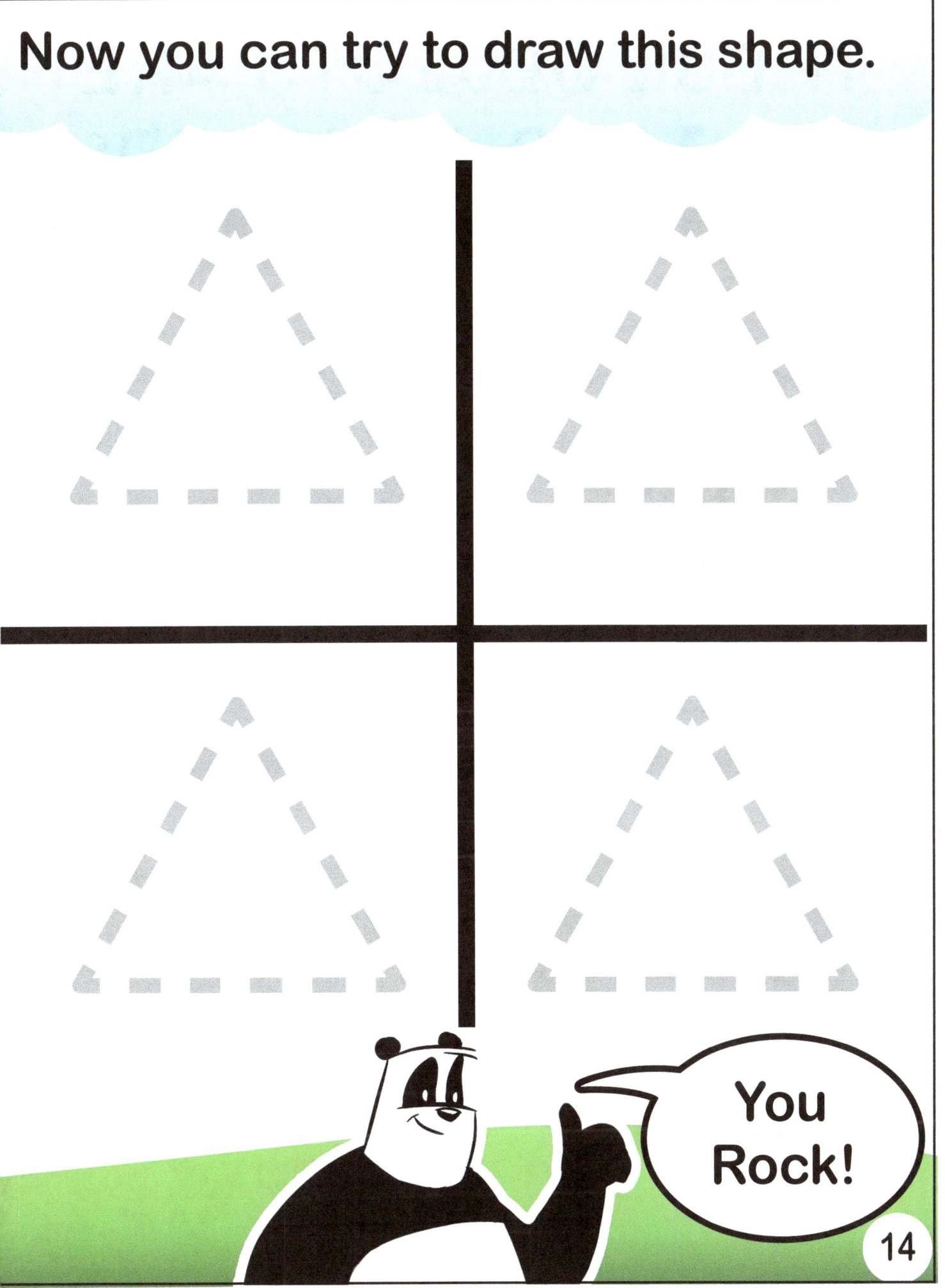

THESE OBJECTS ARE PENTAGON SHAPED:

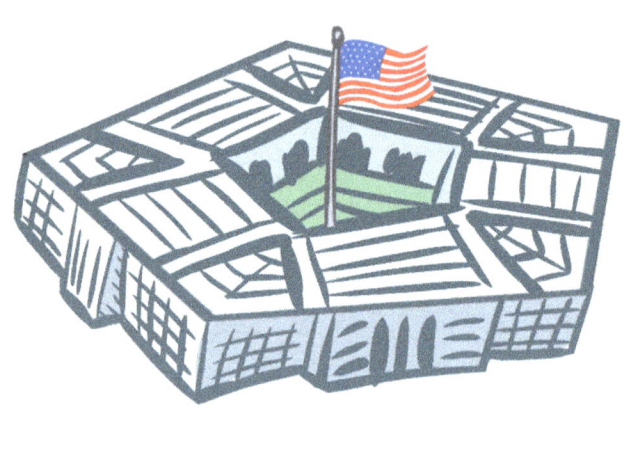

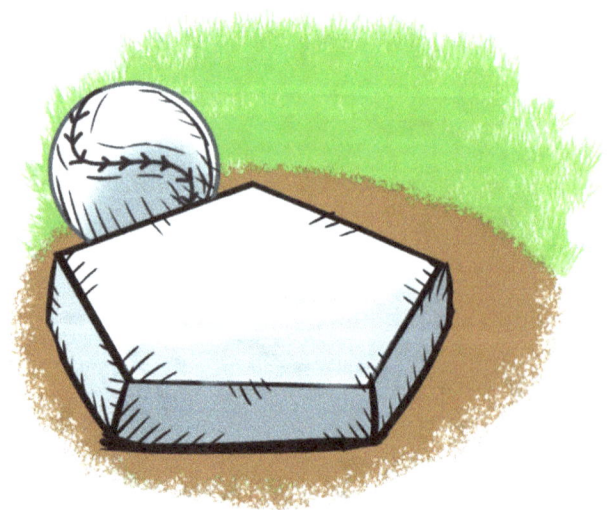

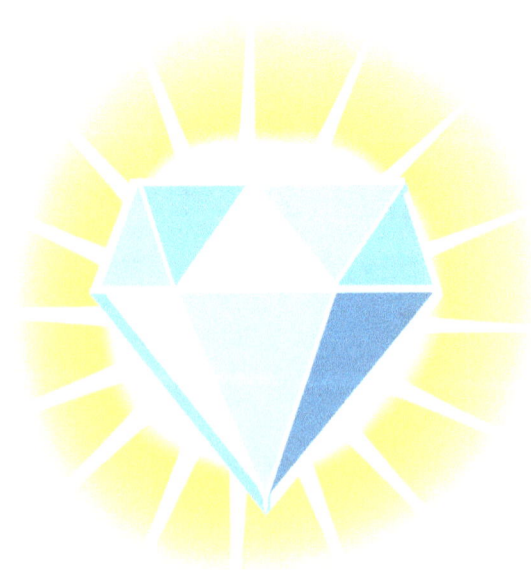

WHAT IS A PENTAGON?

A SHAPE WITH FIVE SIDES AND FIVE ANGLES?

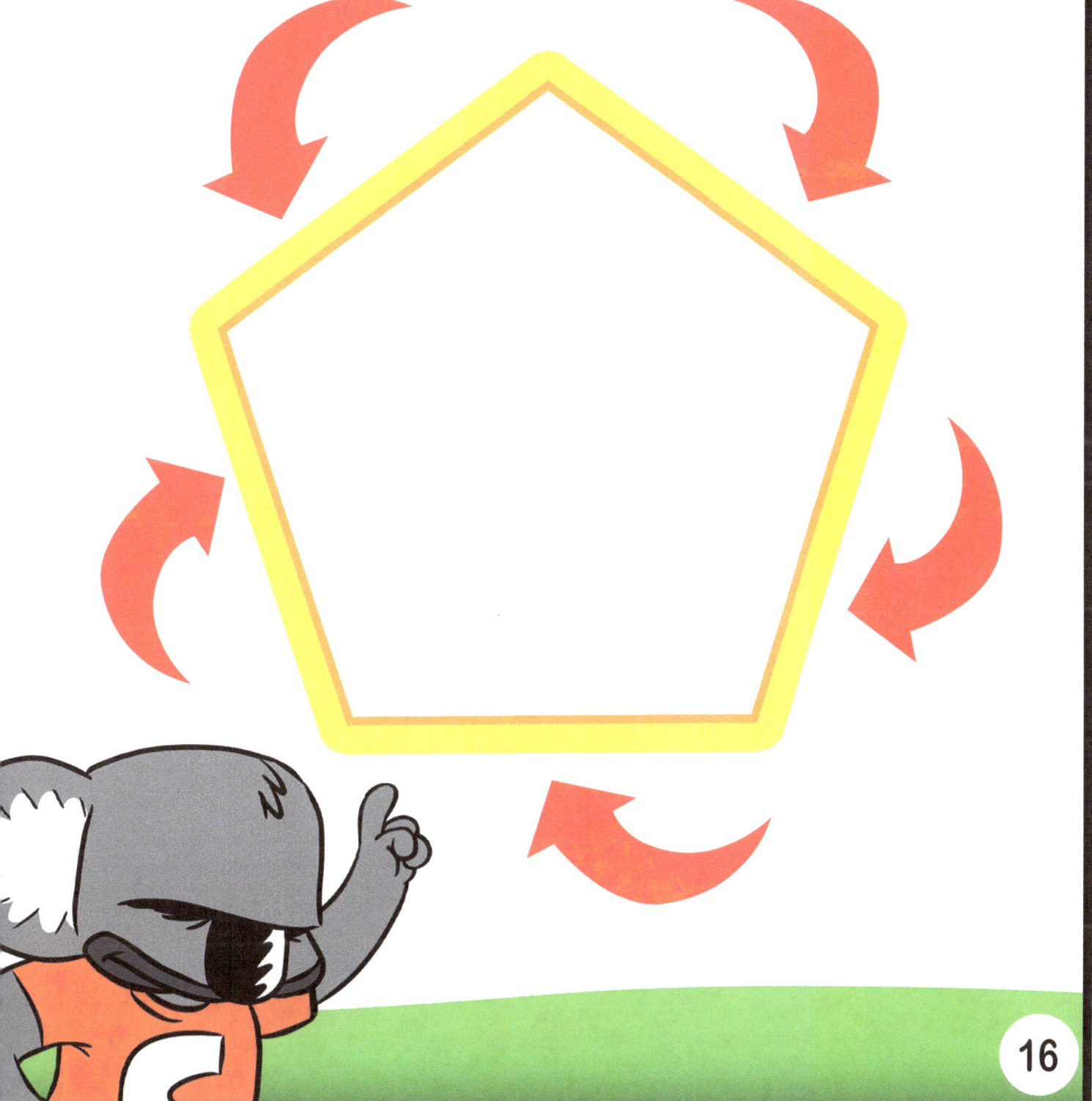

Follow these steps to draw this shape.

1

2

3

4

5

Now you can try to draw this shape.

Excellent!

THESE OBJECTS ARE HALF-CIRCLE SHAPED:

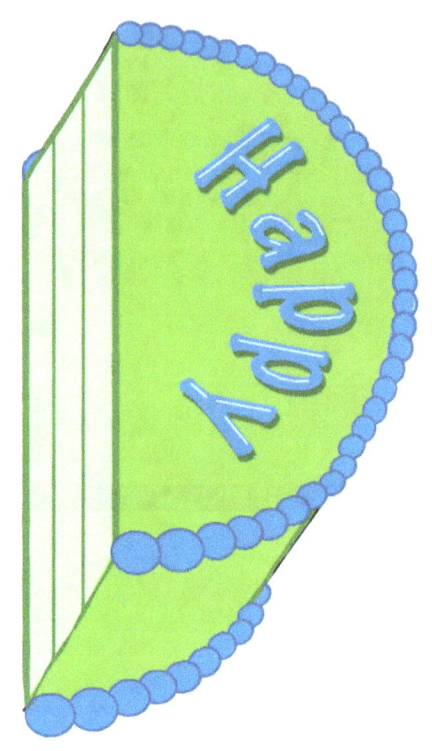

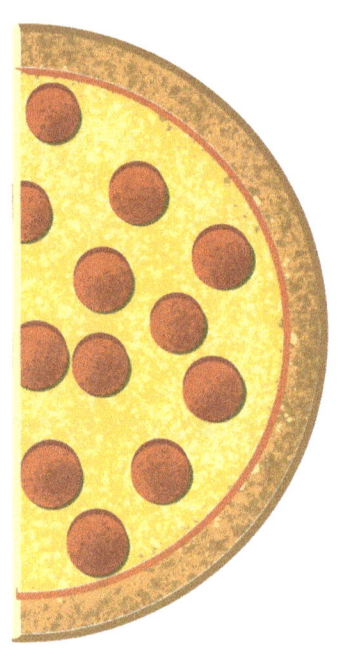

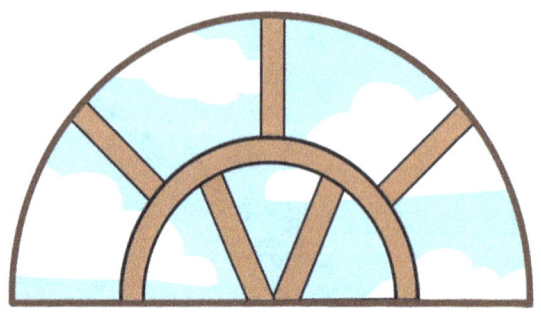

WHAT IS A HALF CIRCLE ?

A SHAPE WITH A FLAT SIDE AND A ROUND SIDE
BY CUTTING A CIRCLE IN HALF RIGHT DOWN THE MIDDLE.

CIRCLE

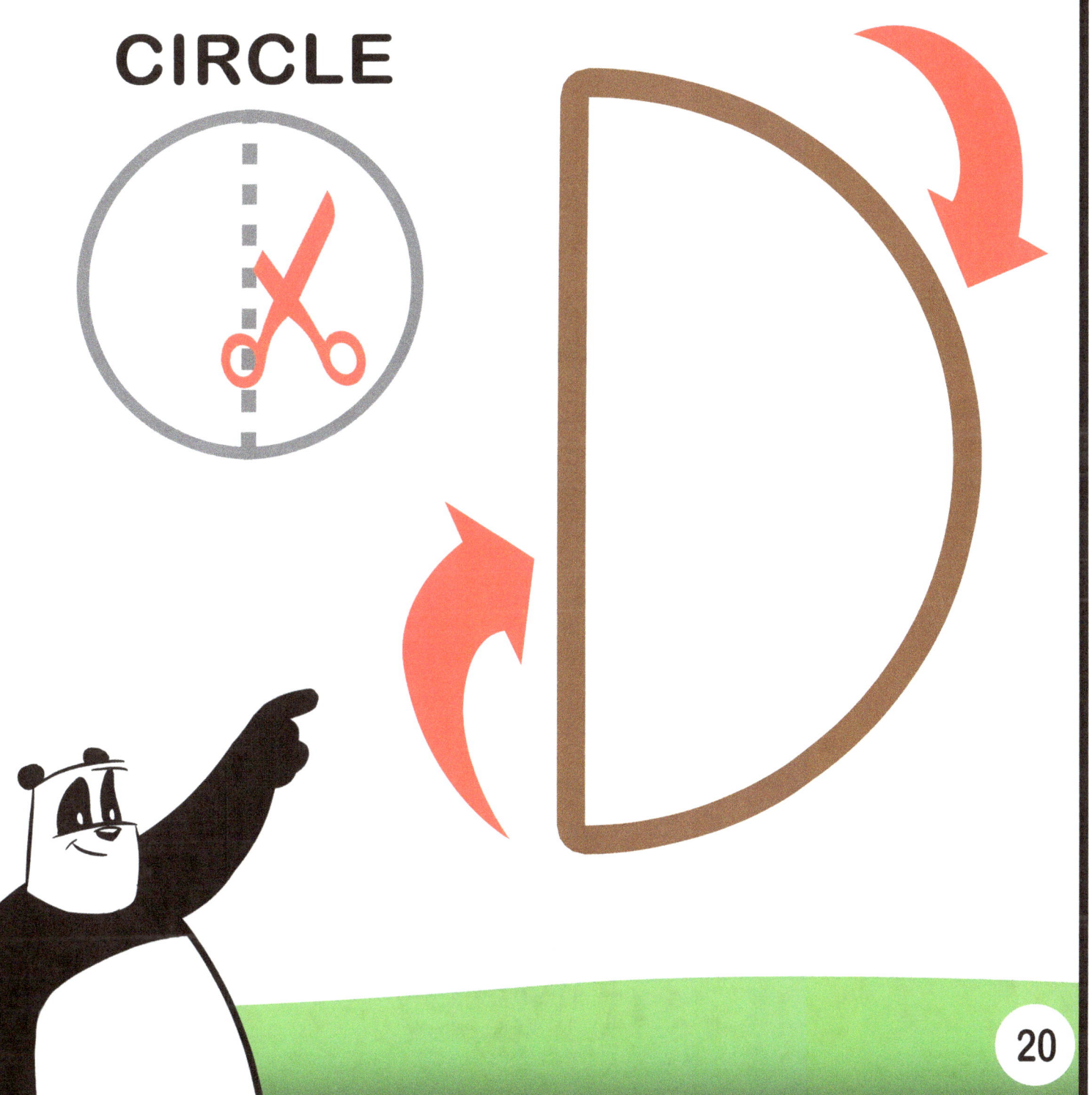

Follow these steps to draw this shape.

1

2

3

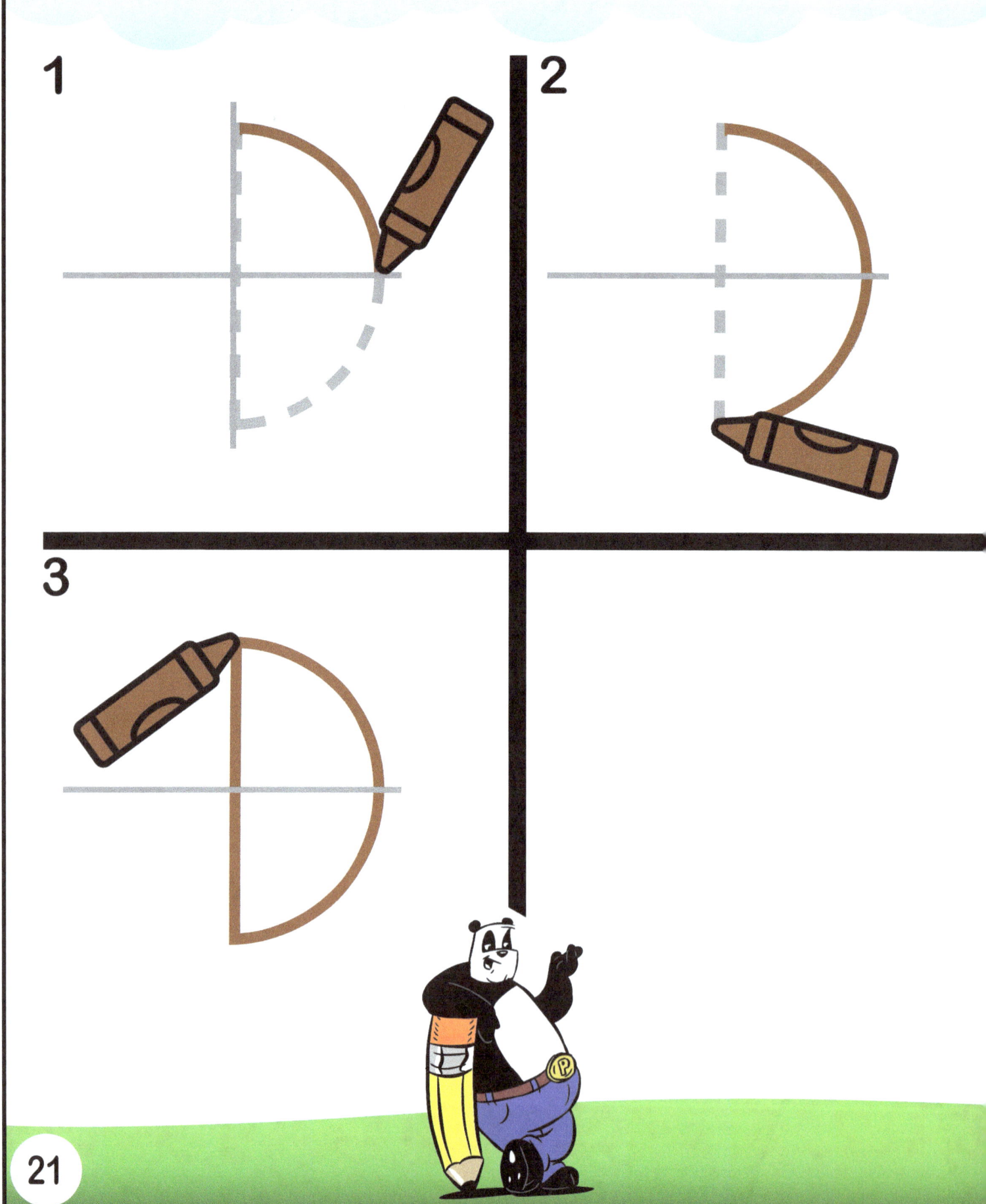

Now you can try to draw this shape.

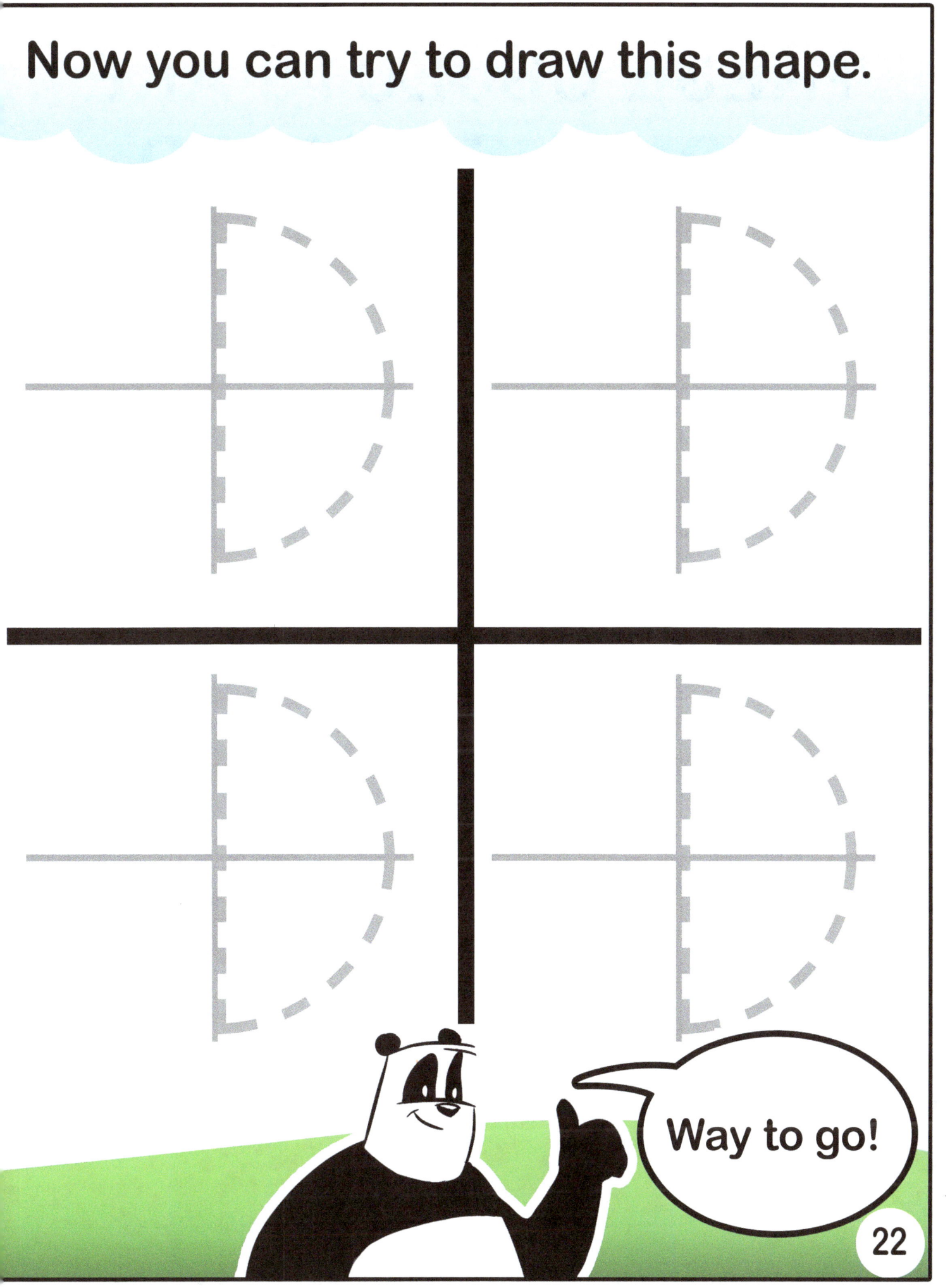

Way to go!

THESE OBJECTS ARE RHOMBUS SHAPED:
(OR DIAMOND SHAPE)

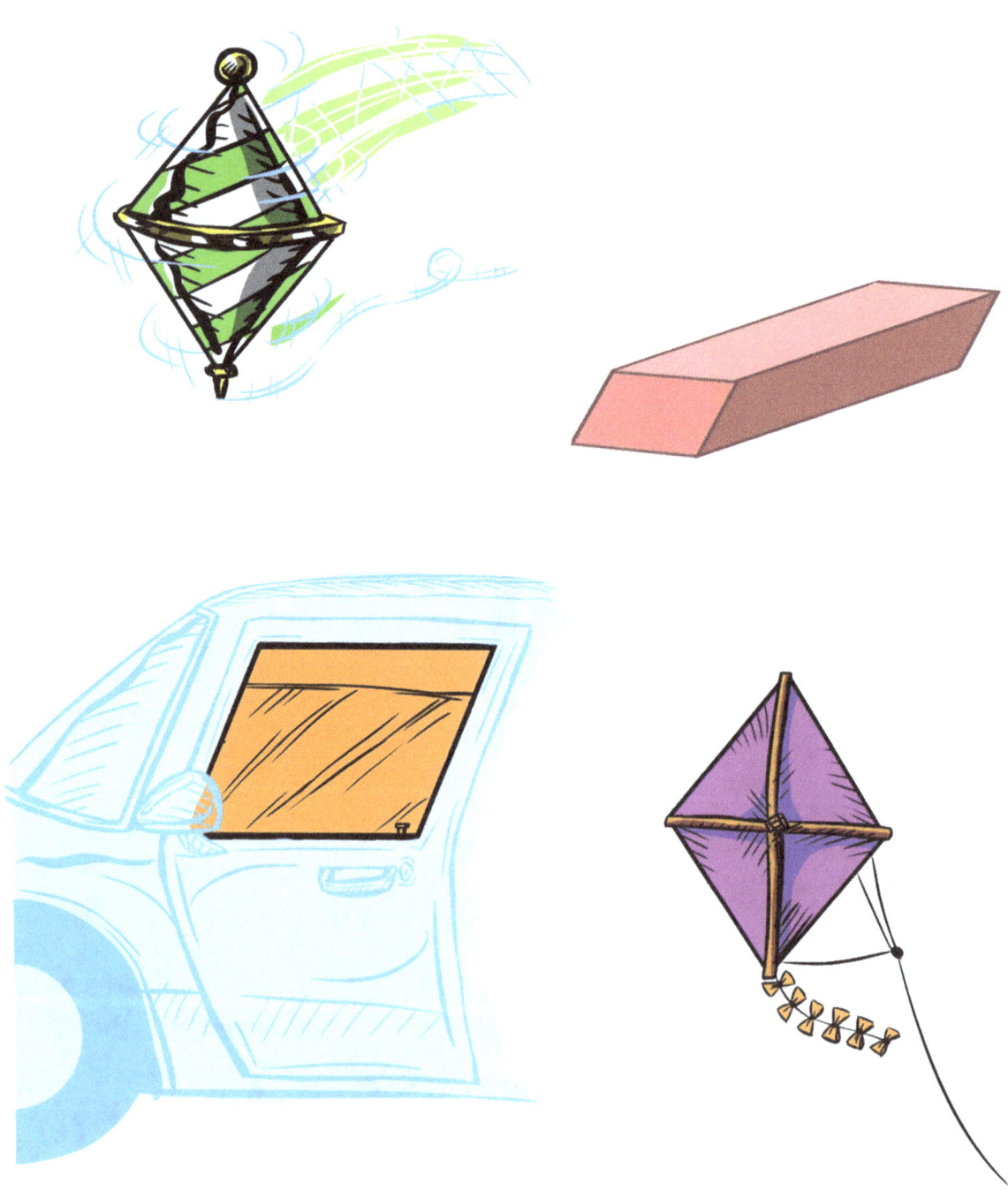

WHAT IS A RHOMBUS?

A SQUARE SHAPE WITH TWO STRAIGHT AND TWO SLANTED SIDES.

SQUARE

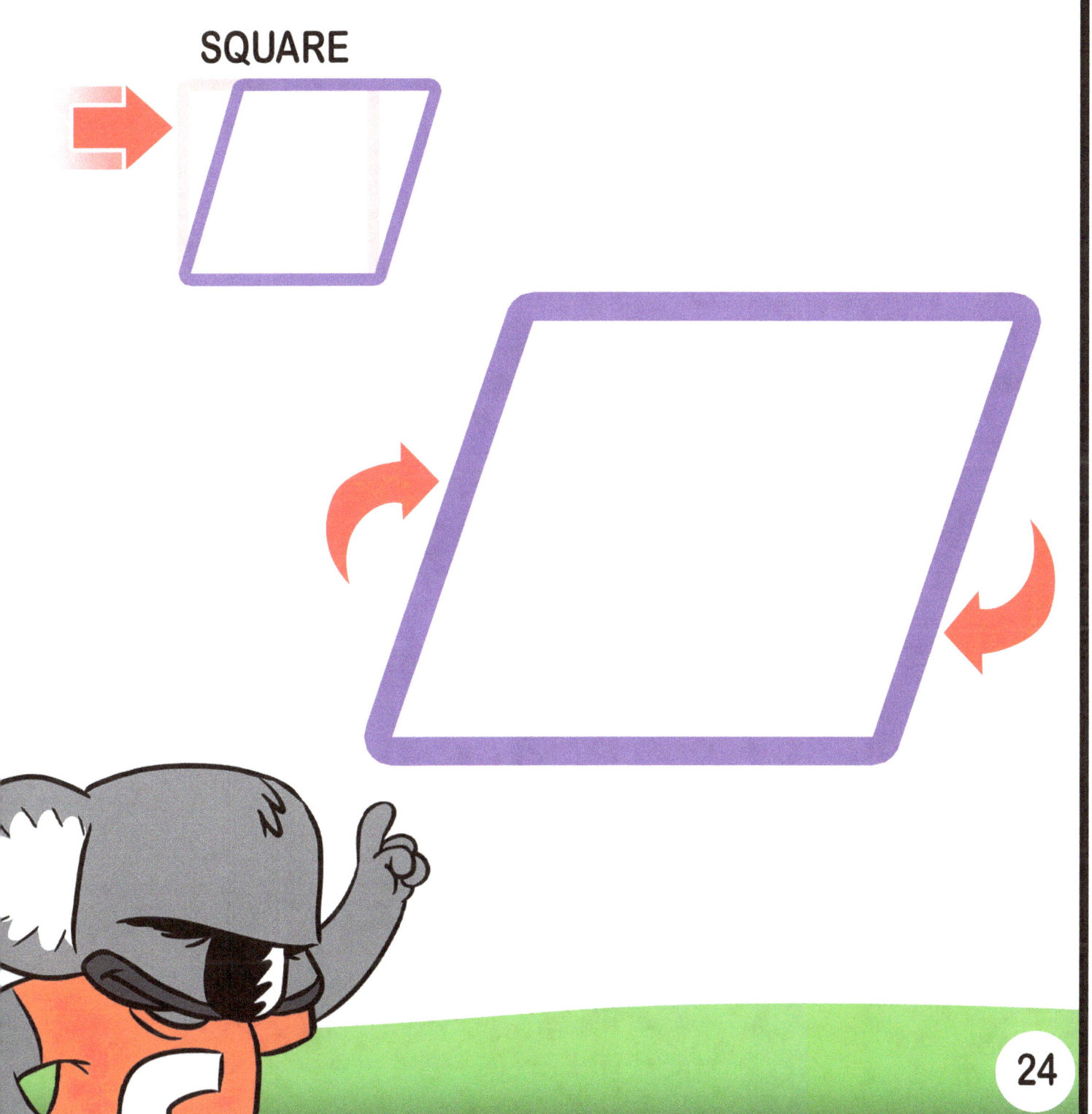

Follow these steps to draw this shape.

1

2

3

4

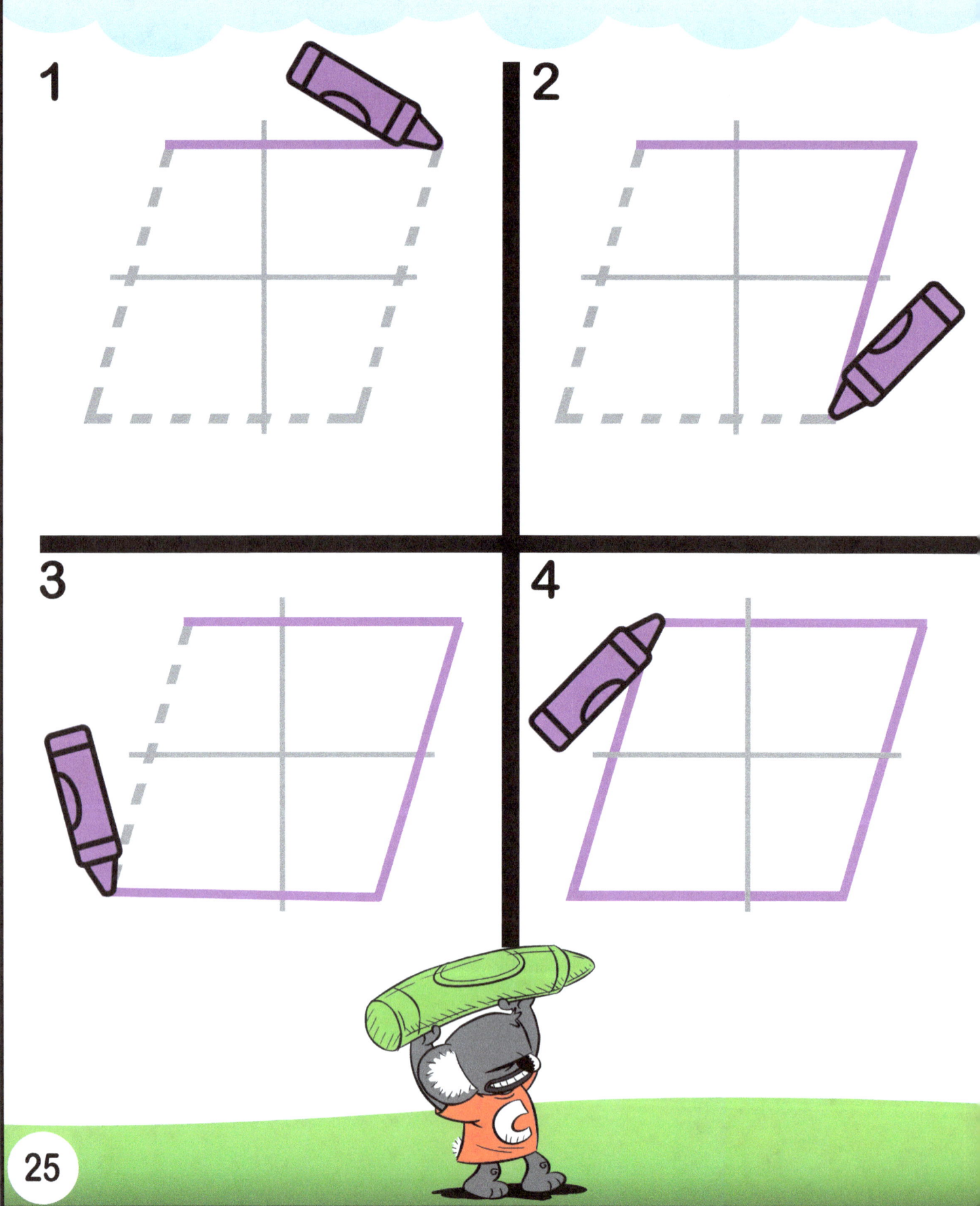

Now you can try to draw this shape.

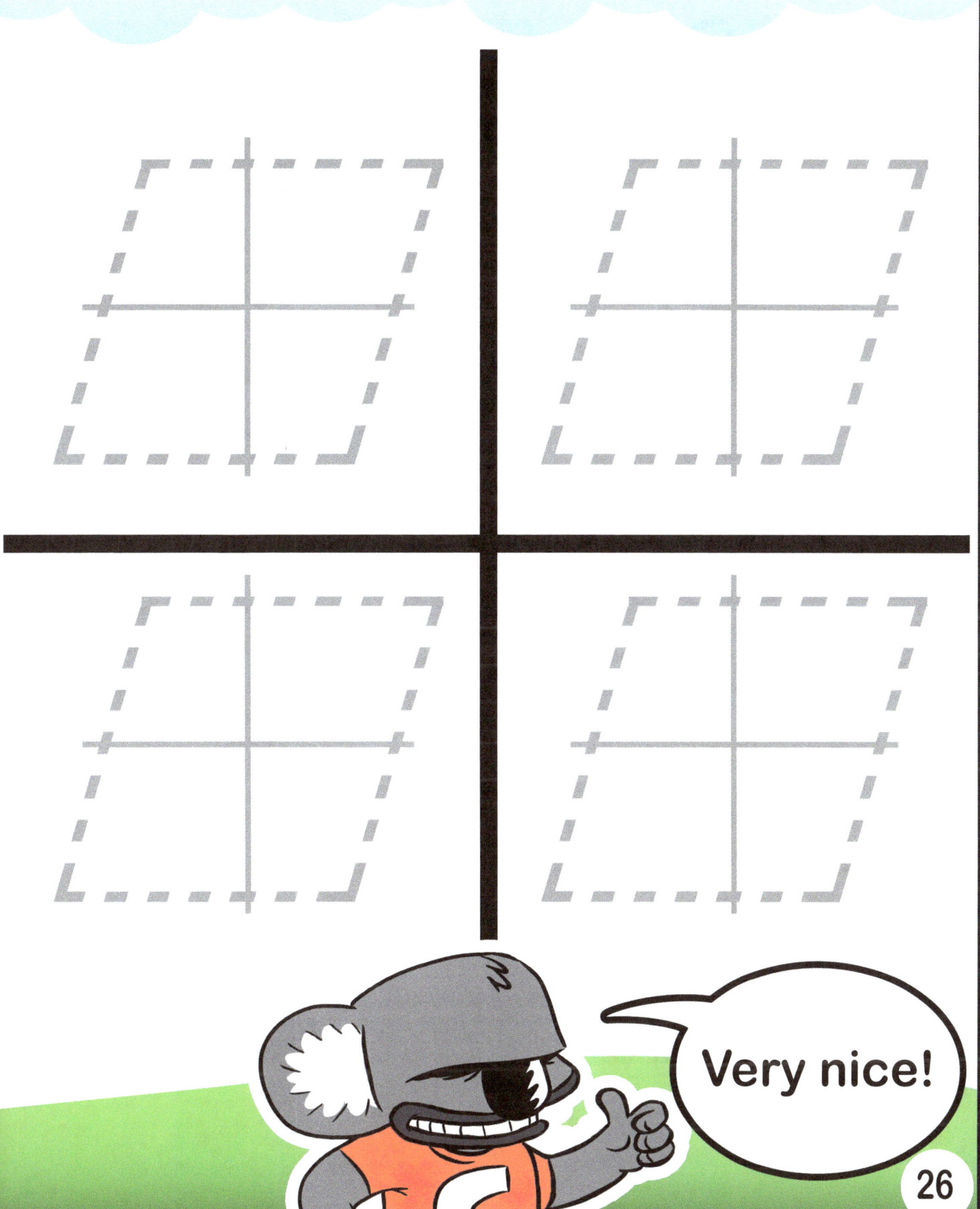

Very nice!

26

THESE OBJECTS ARE MOON SHAPED:
(OR CRESCENT)

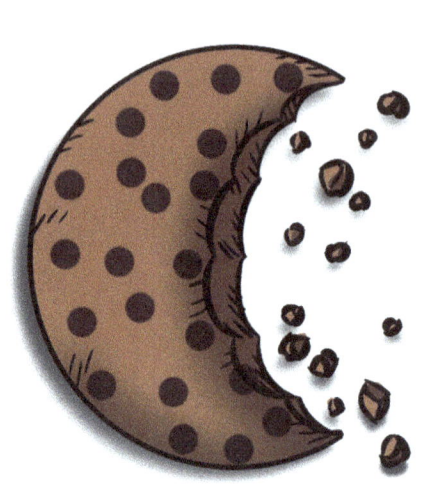 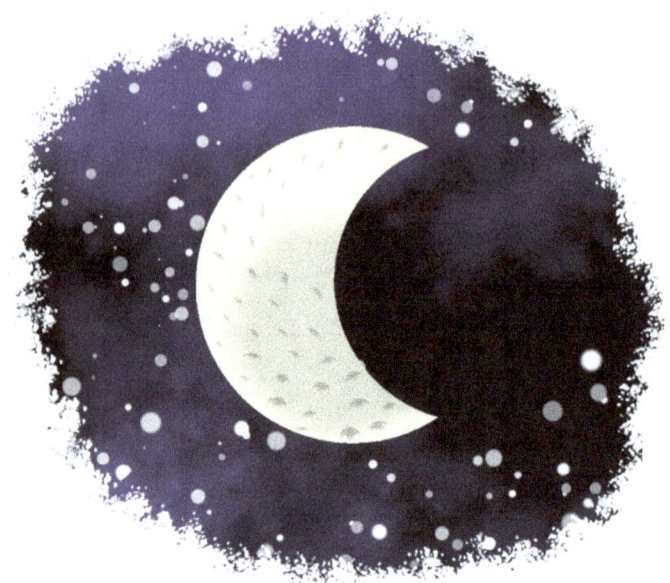

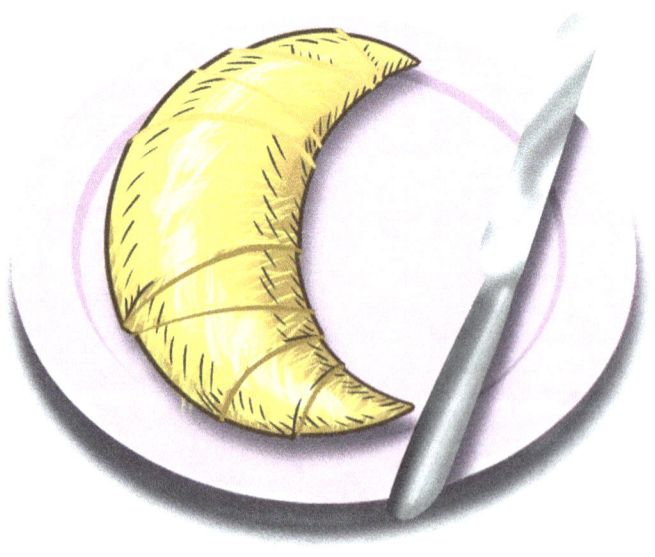 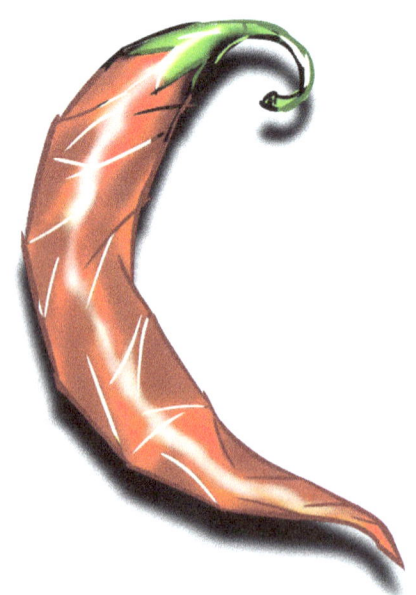

WHAT IS A MOON SHAPE ?

A SHAPE MADE BY REMOVING A SMALL ROUND PART FROM THE CORNER OF A CIRCLE SHAPE.

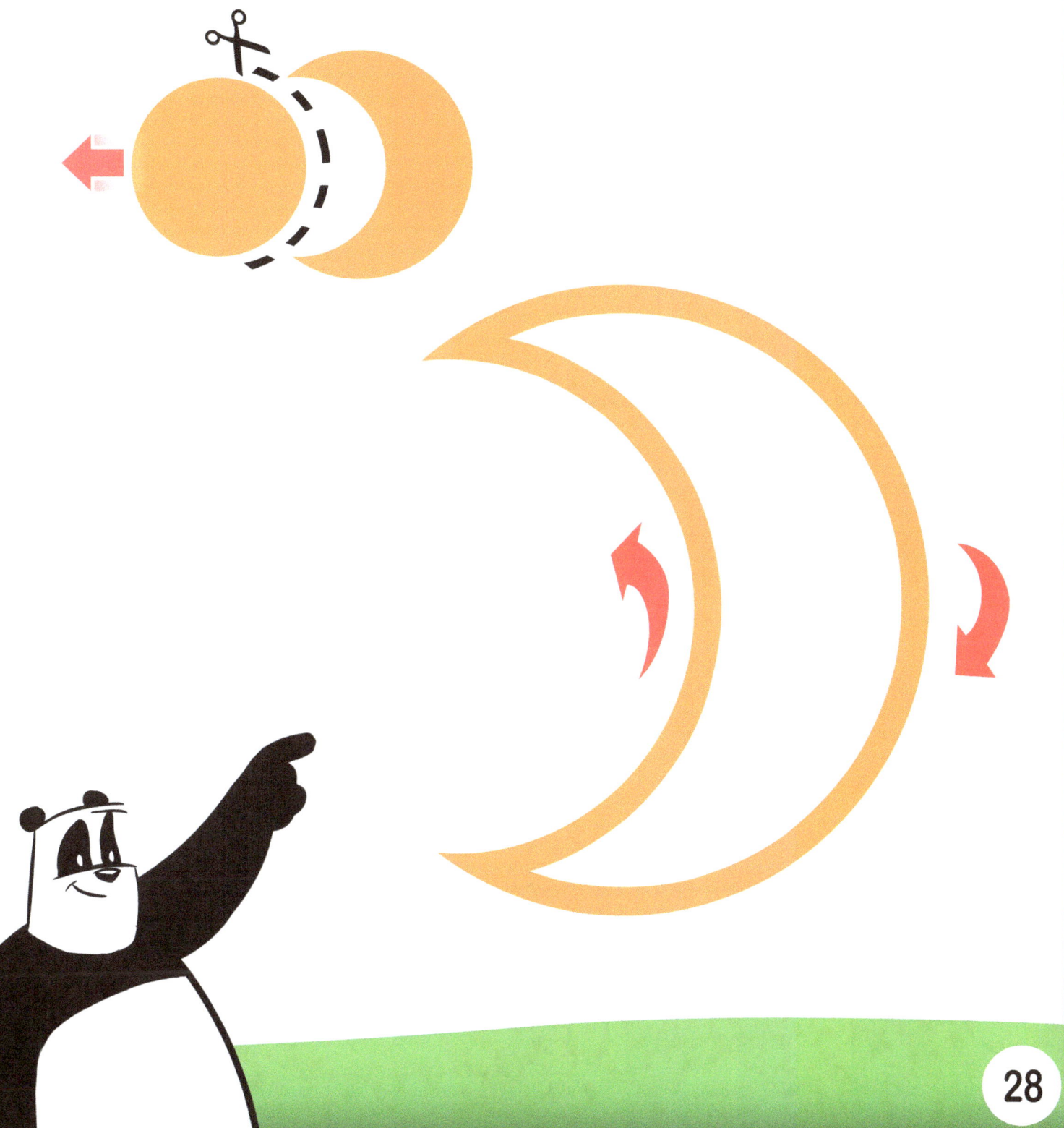

Follow these steps to draw this shape.

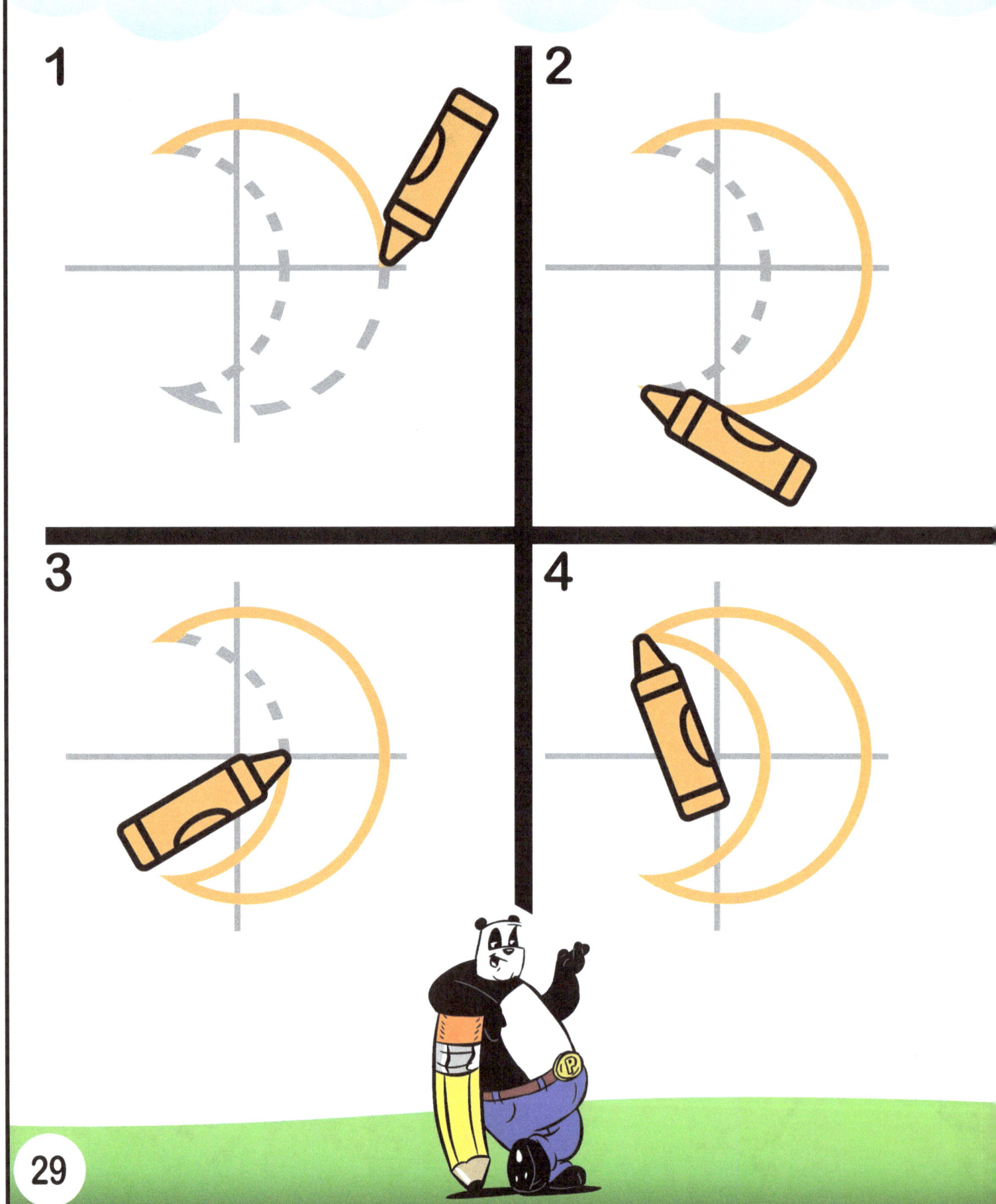

1

2

3

4

Now you can try to draw this shape.

Fantastic!

THESE OBJECTS ARE RECTANGLE SHAPED:

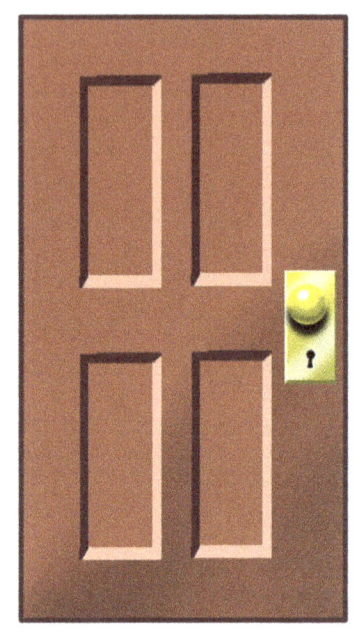

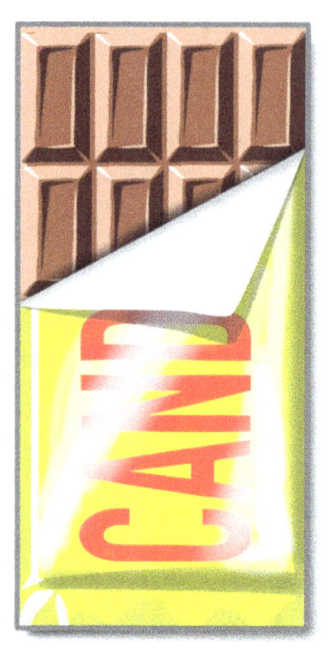

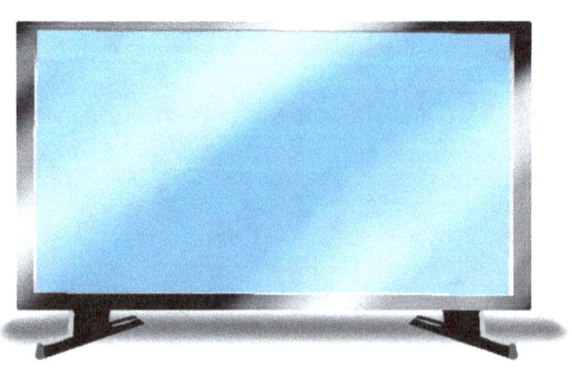

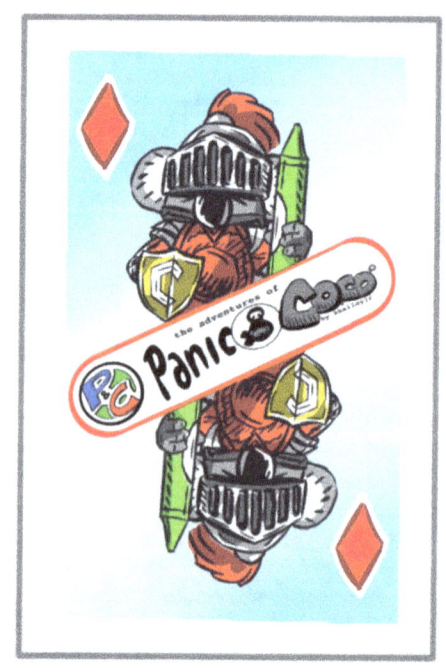

WHAT IS A RECTANGLE?

A SQUARE SHAPE WITH TWO SHORT SIDES AND TWO LONG SIDES.

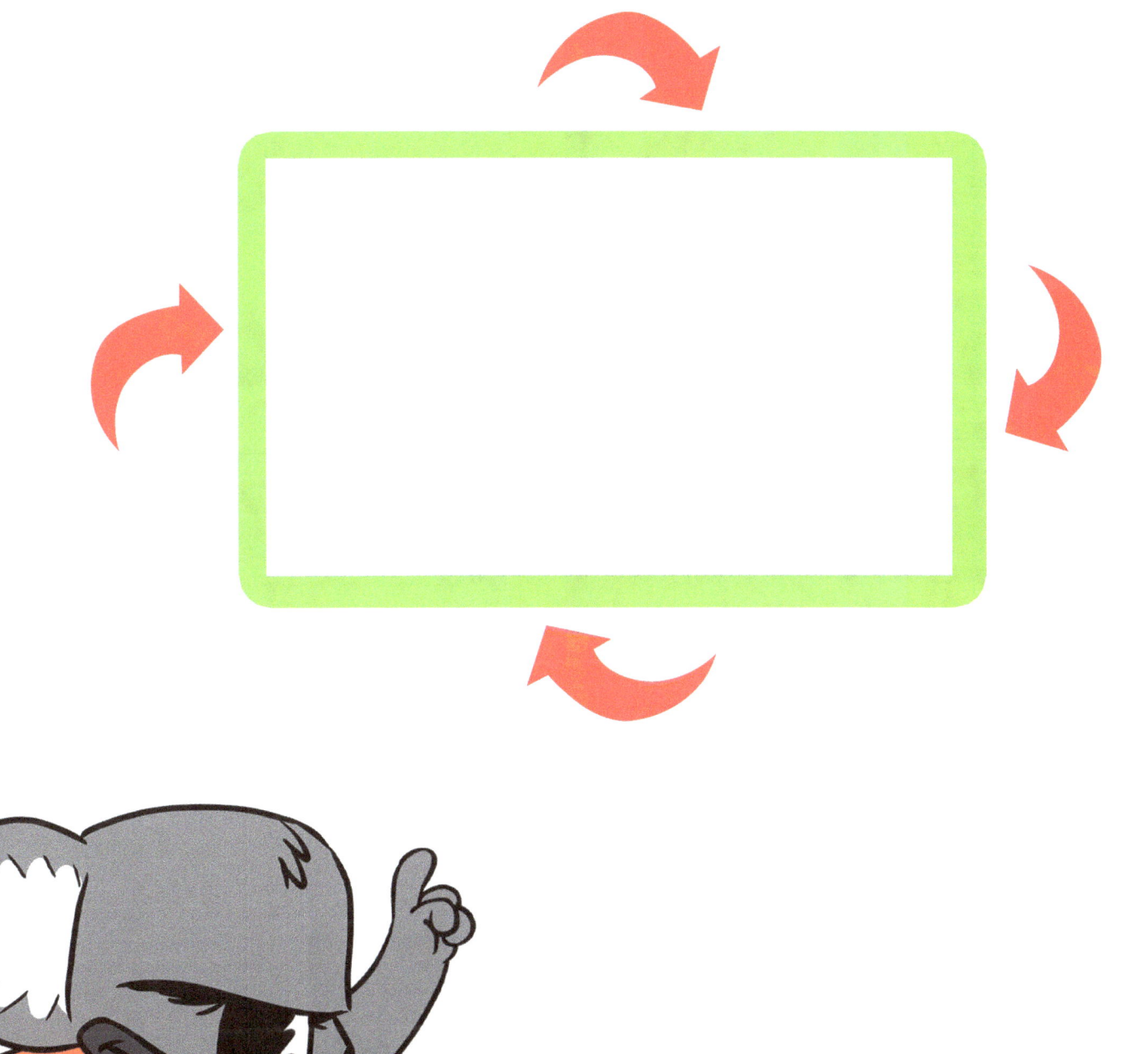

Follow these steps to draw this shape.

1

2

3

4

Now you can try to draw this shape.

Keep it up!

THESE OBJECTS ARE OVAL SHAPED:

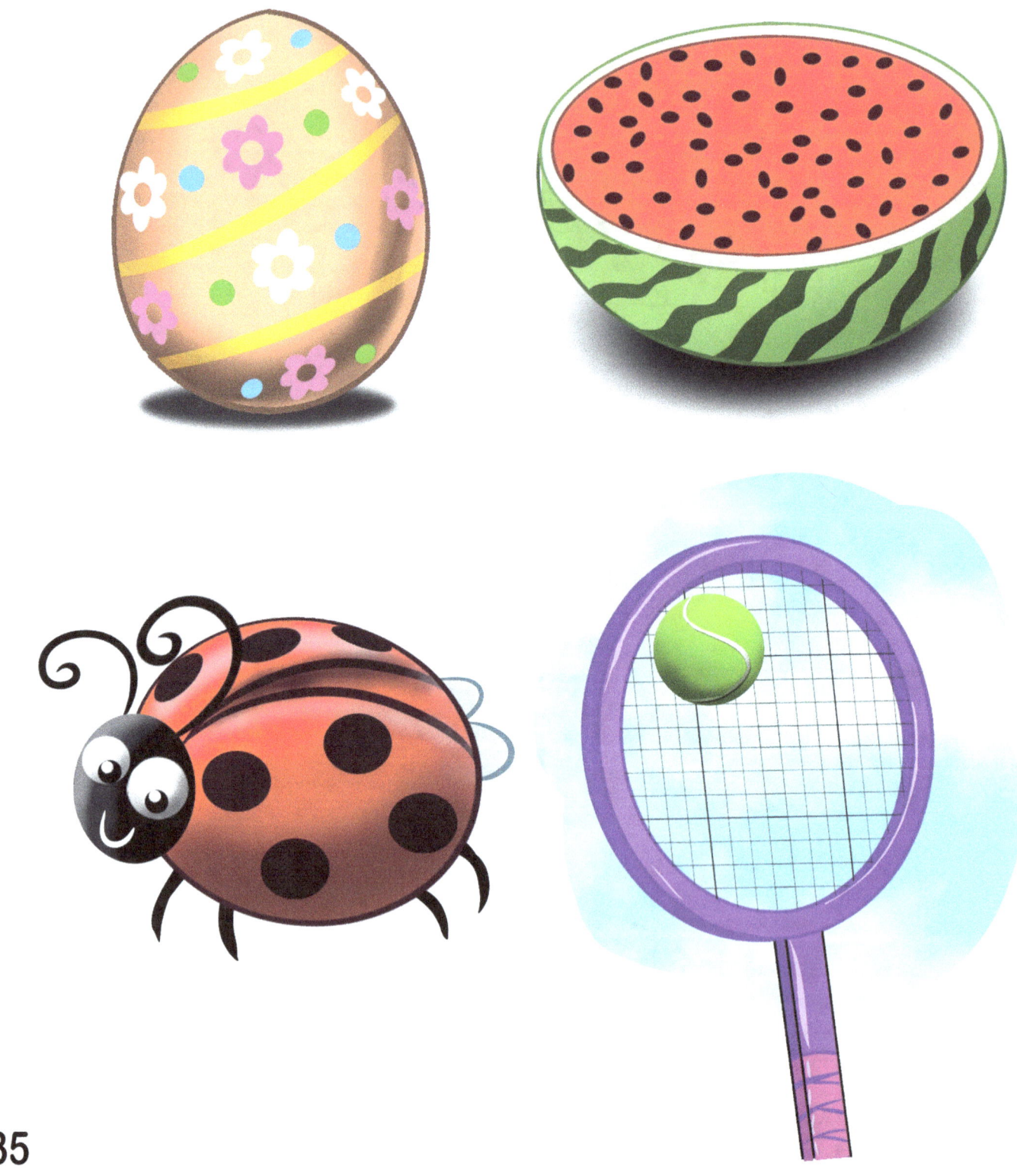

WHAT IS AN OVAL ?

A ROUND SHAPE THAT LOOKS LIKE A STRETCHED CIRCLE.

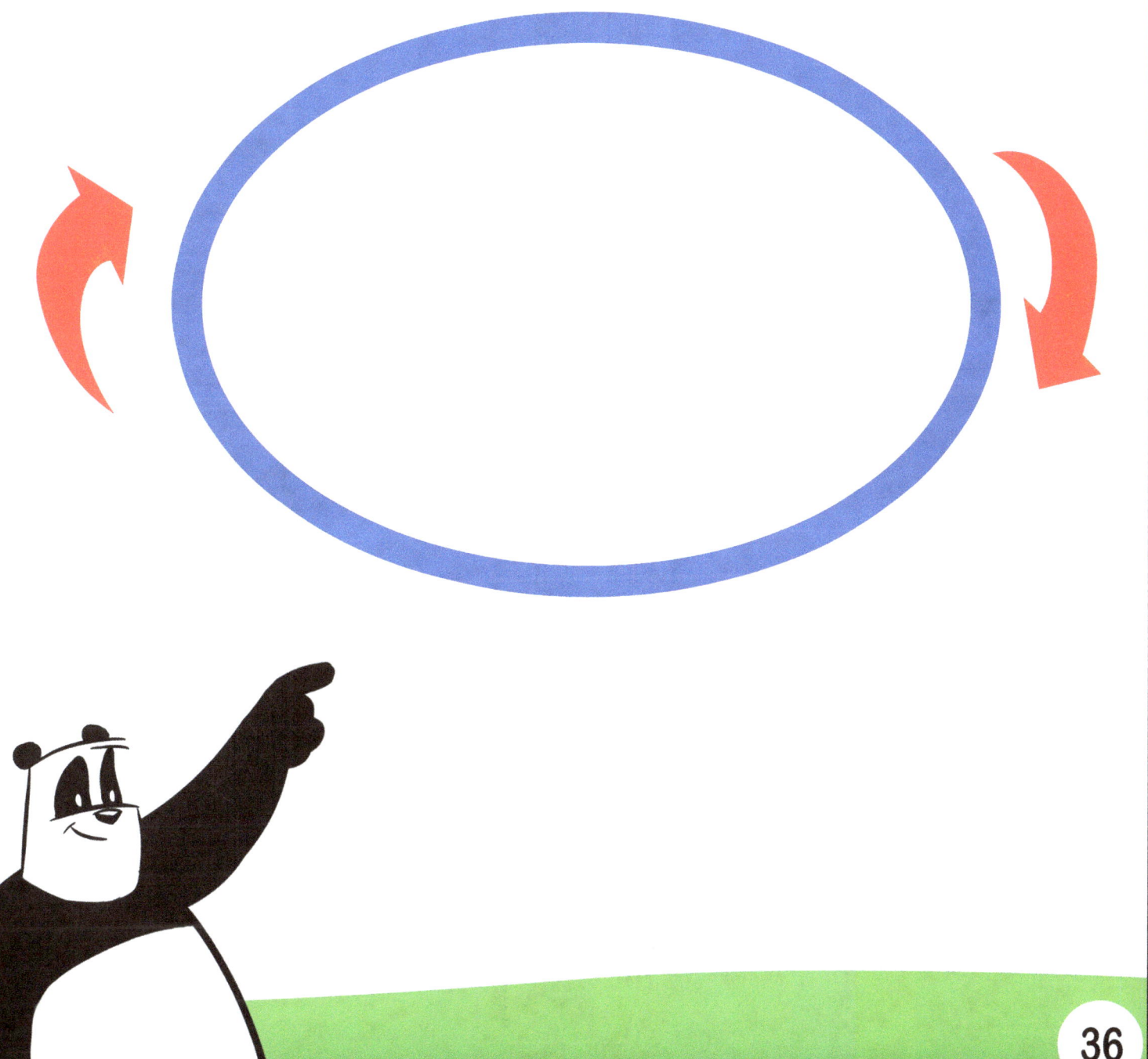

Follow these steps to draw this shape.

1

2

3

4

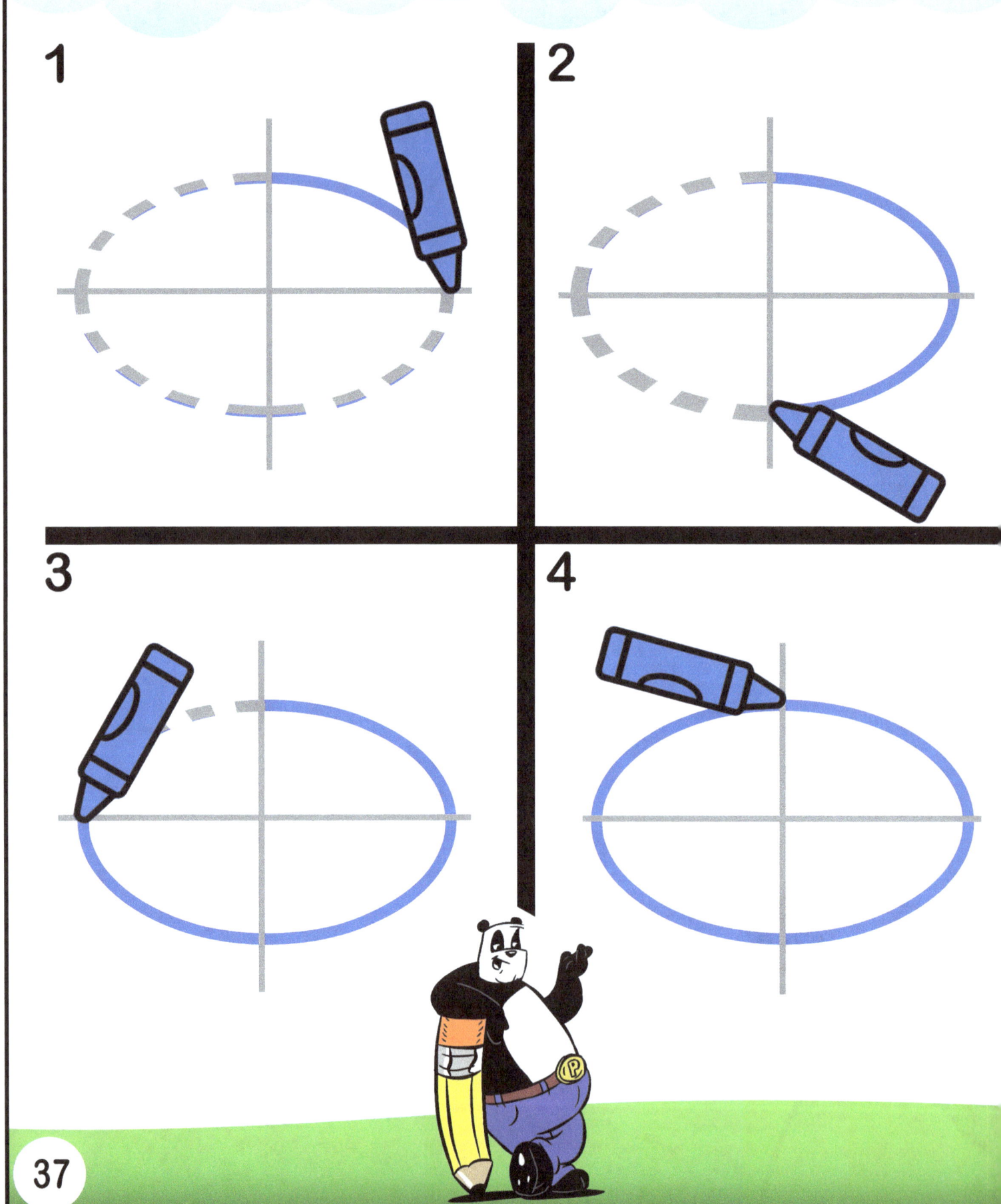

Now you can try to draw this shape.

Looks good to me!

THESE OBJECTS ARE HEART SHAPED:

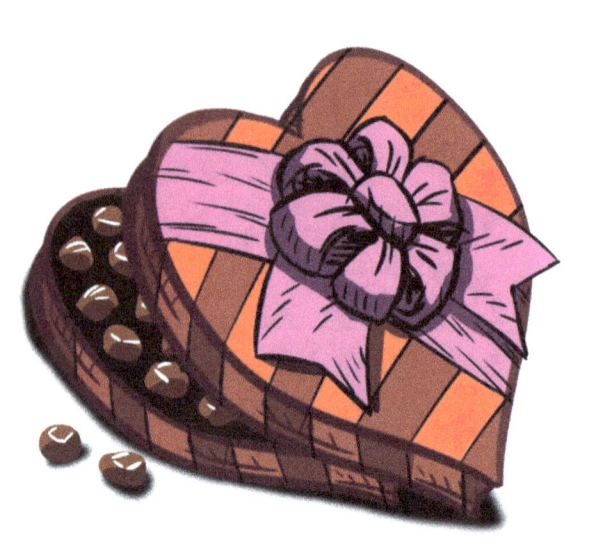

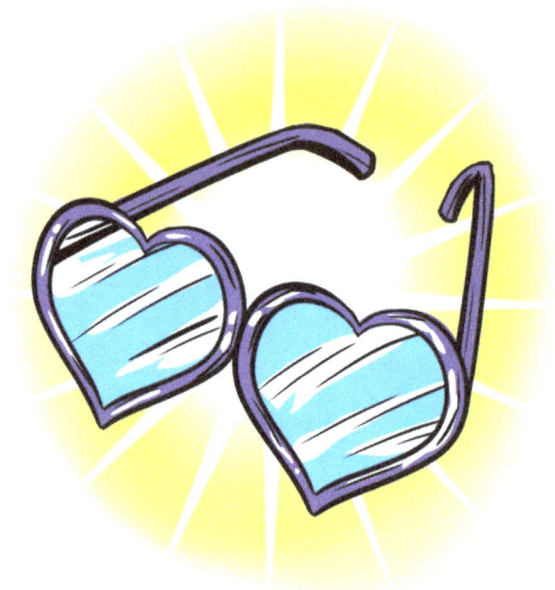

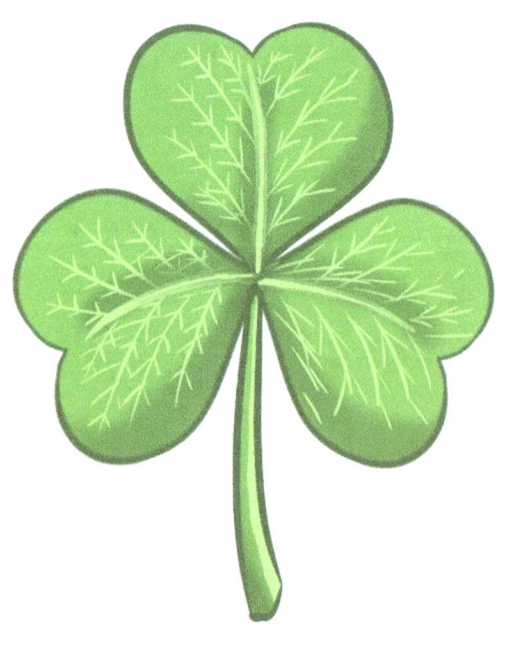

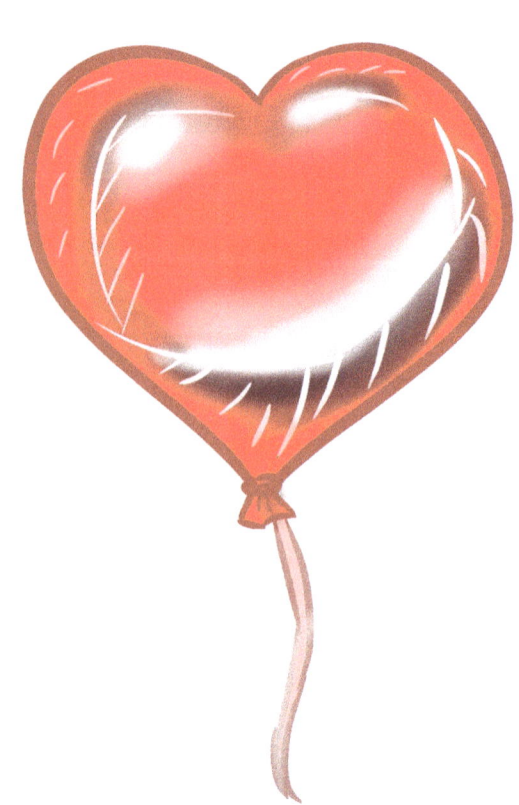

WHAT IS A HEART SHAPE?

A HEART SHAPE CAN BE MADE BY COMBINING TWO CIRCLES AND ONE TRIANGLE.

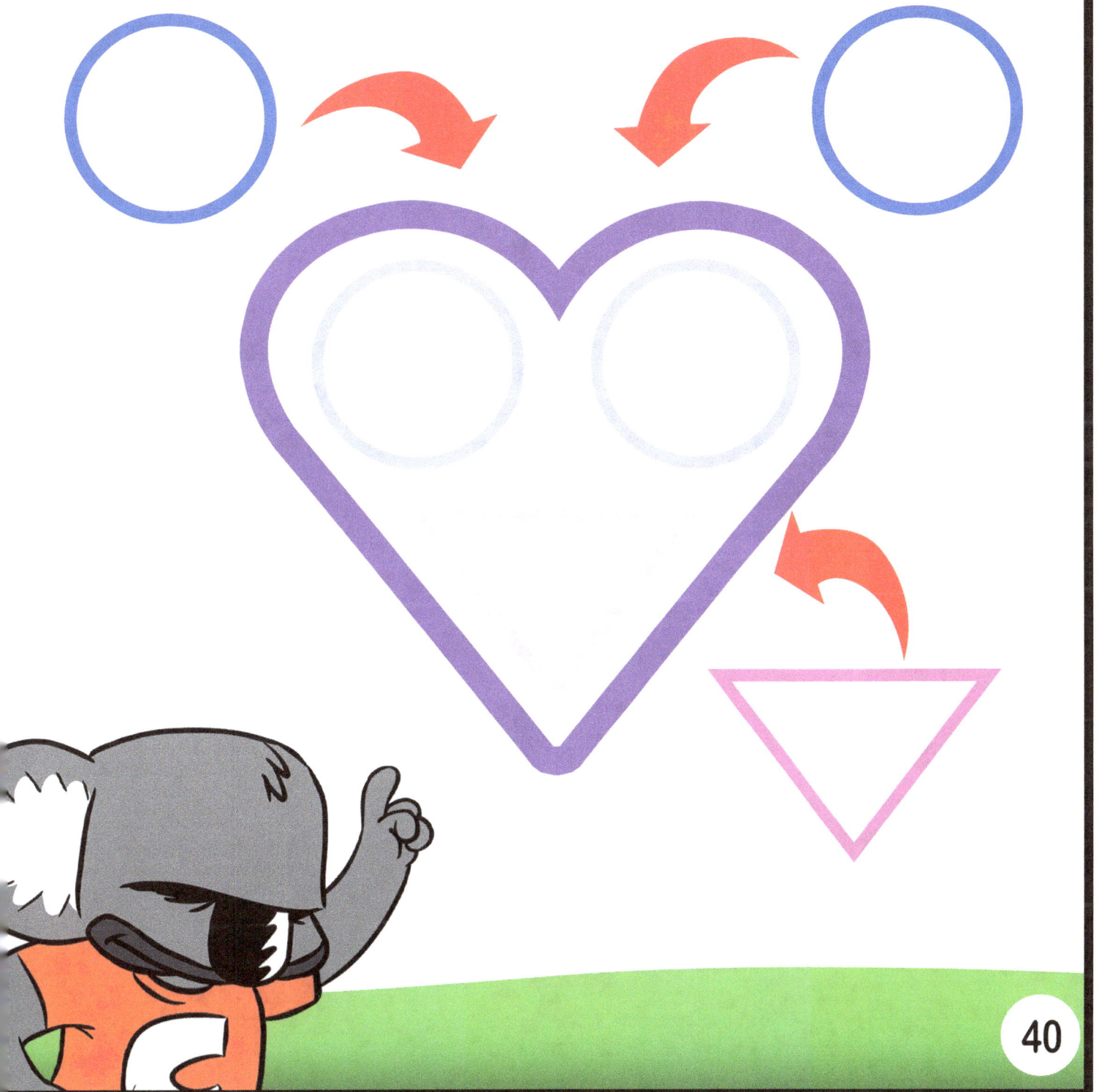

Follow these steps to draw this shape.

1

2

3

4

Now you can try to draw this shape.

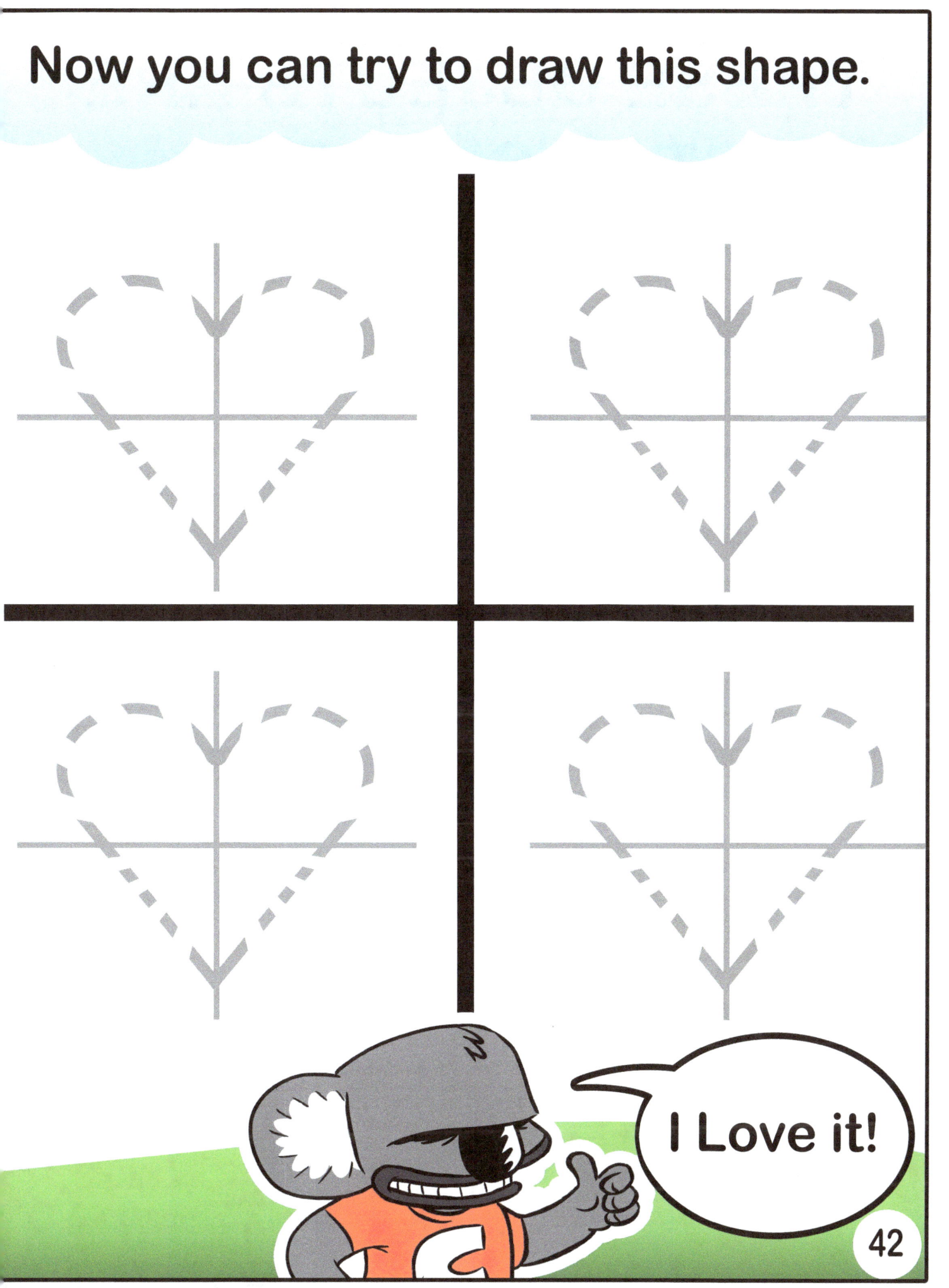

THESE OBJECTS ARE STAR SHAPED:

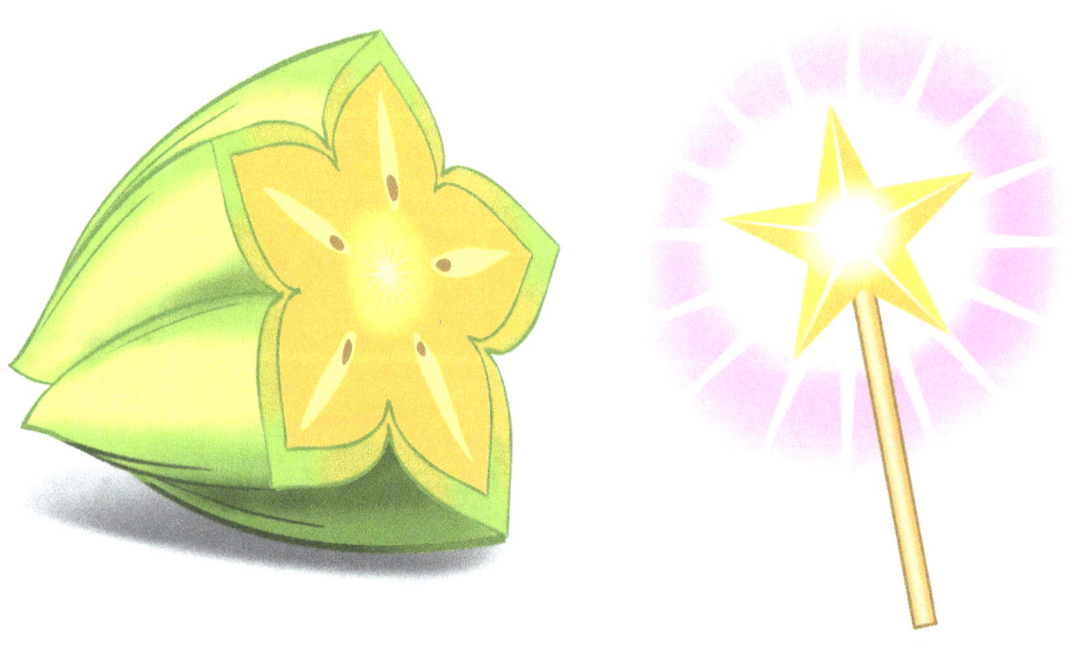

WHAT IS A STAR SHAPE?

YOU CAN COMBINE FIVE TRIANGLES AND ONE PENTAGON.

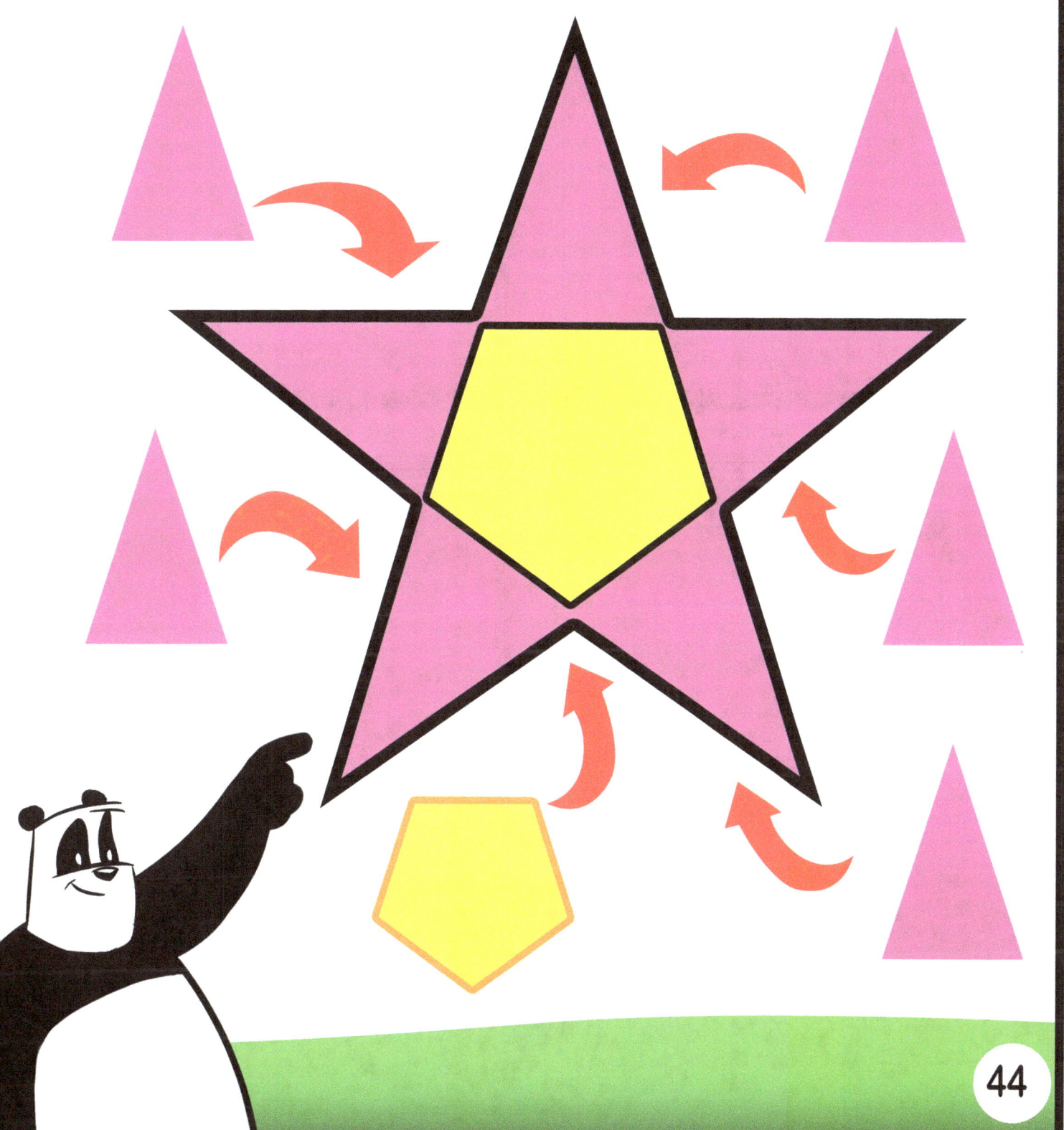

Follow these steps to draw this shape.

1

2

3

4

Now you can try to draw this shape.

Cool drawing!

THESE OBJECTS ARE ARROW SHAPED:

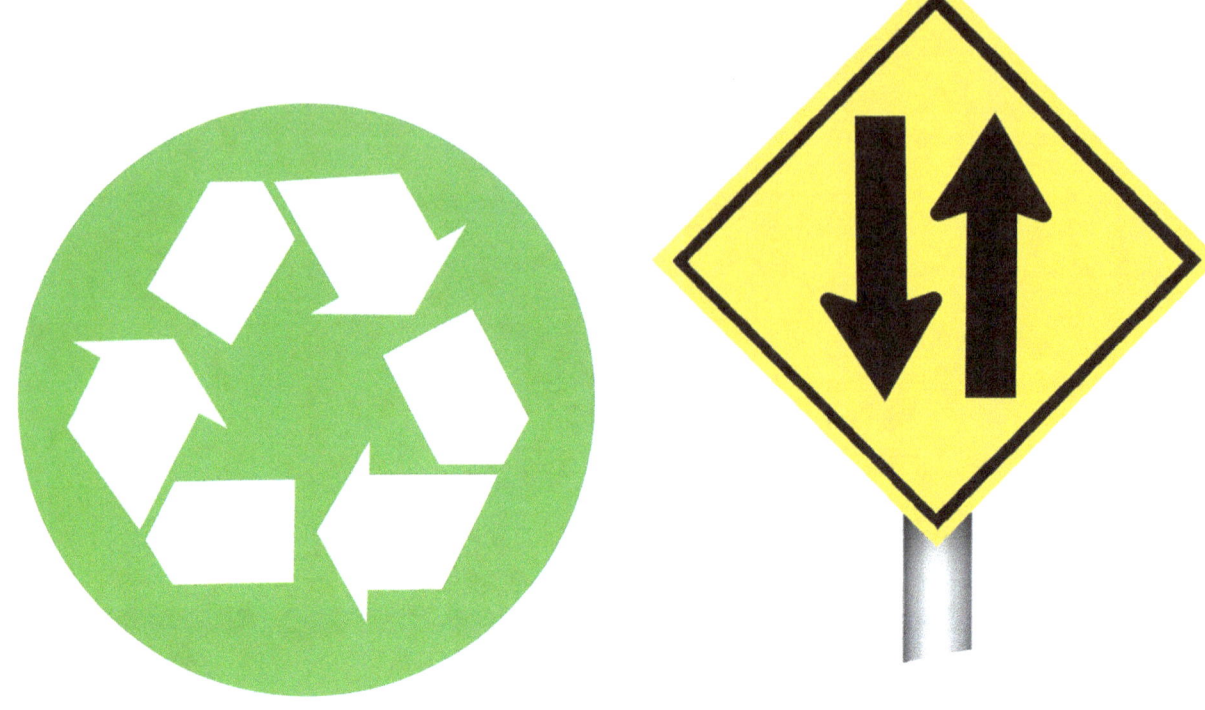

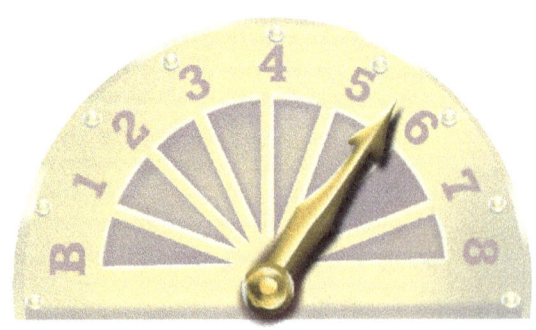

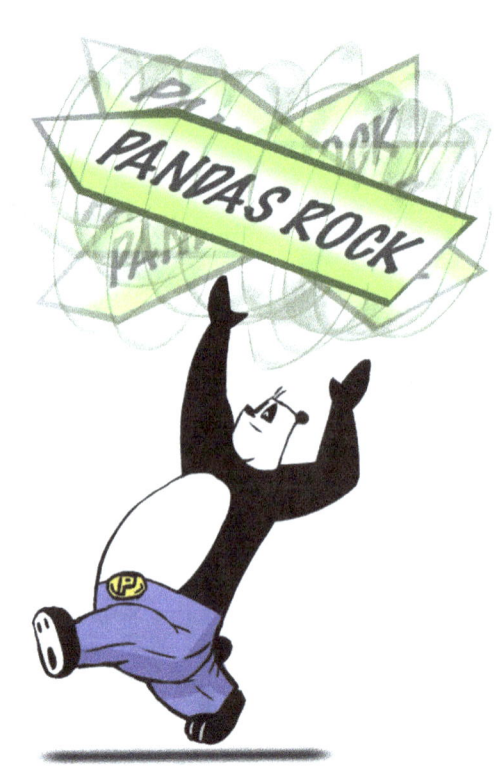

WHAT IS AN ARROW?

IT CAN BE MADE BY COMBINING RECTANGLE AND TRIANGLE.

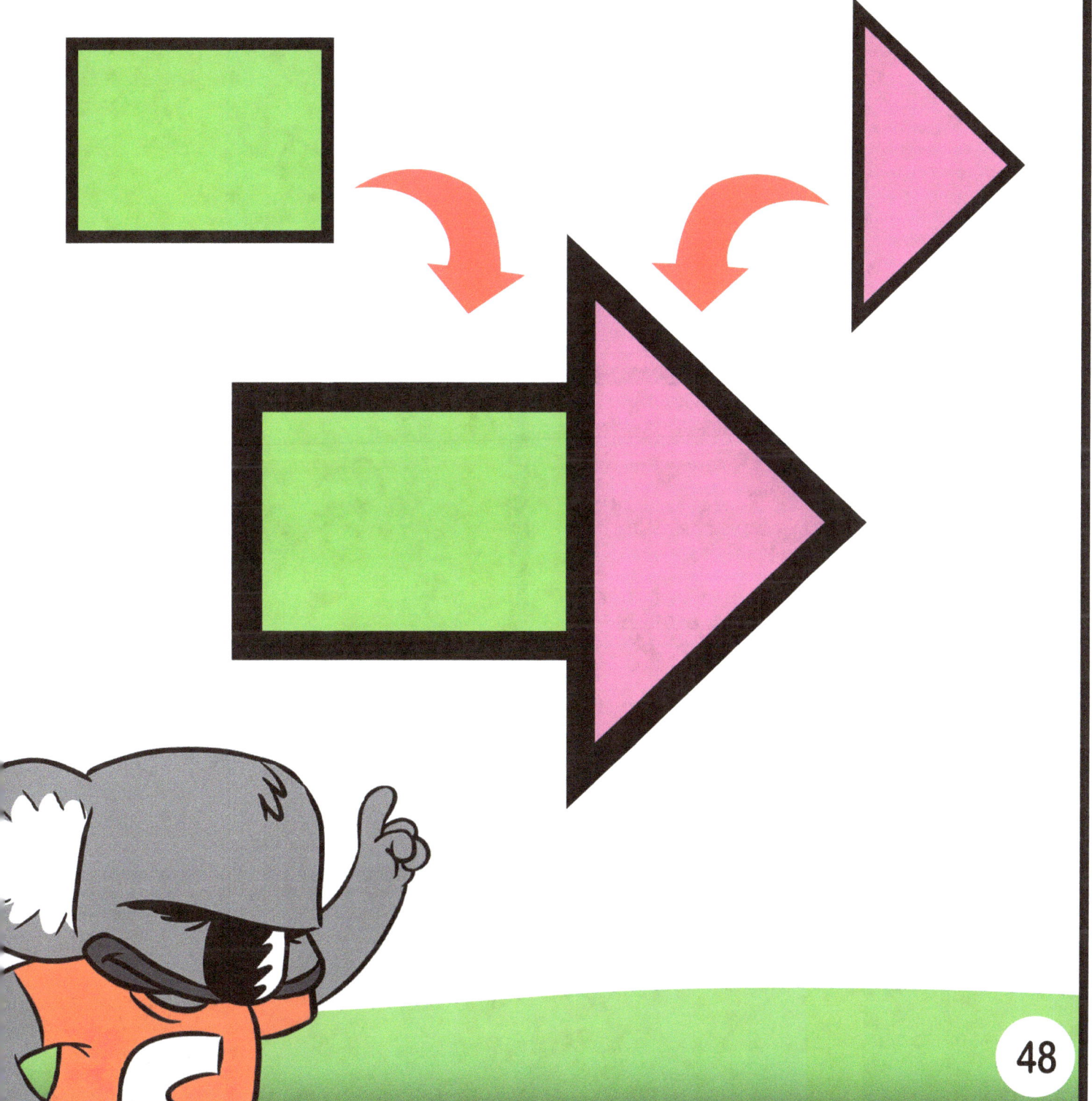

Follow these steps to draw this shape.

1

2

3

4

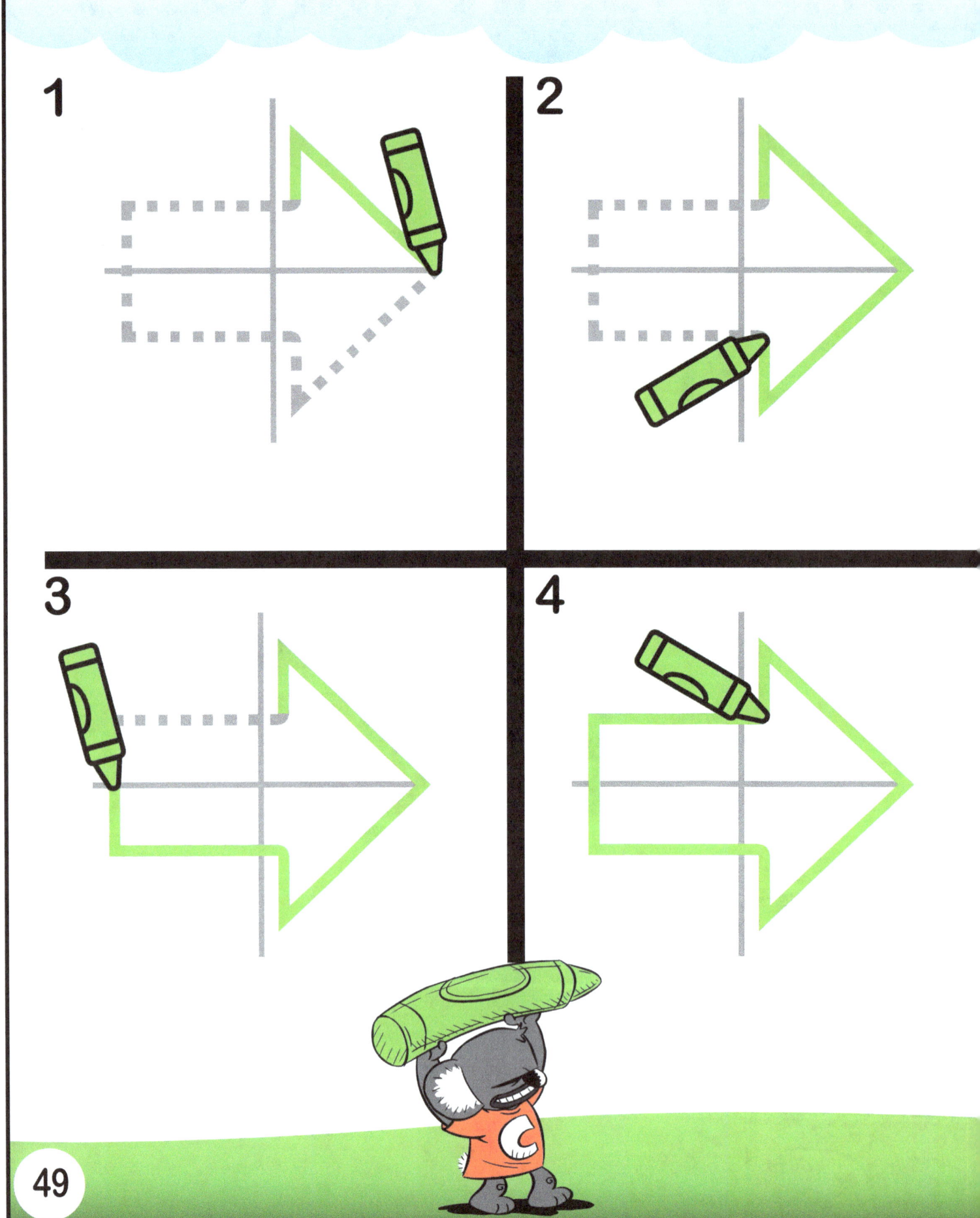

Now you can try to draw this shape.

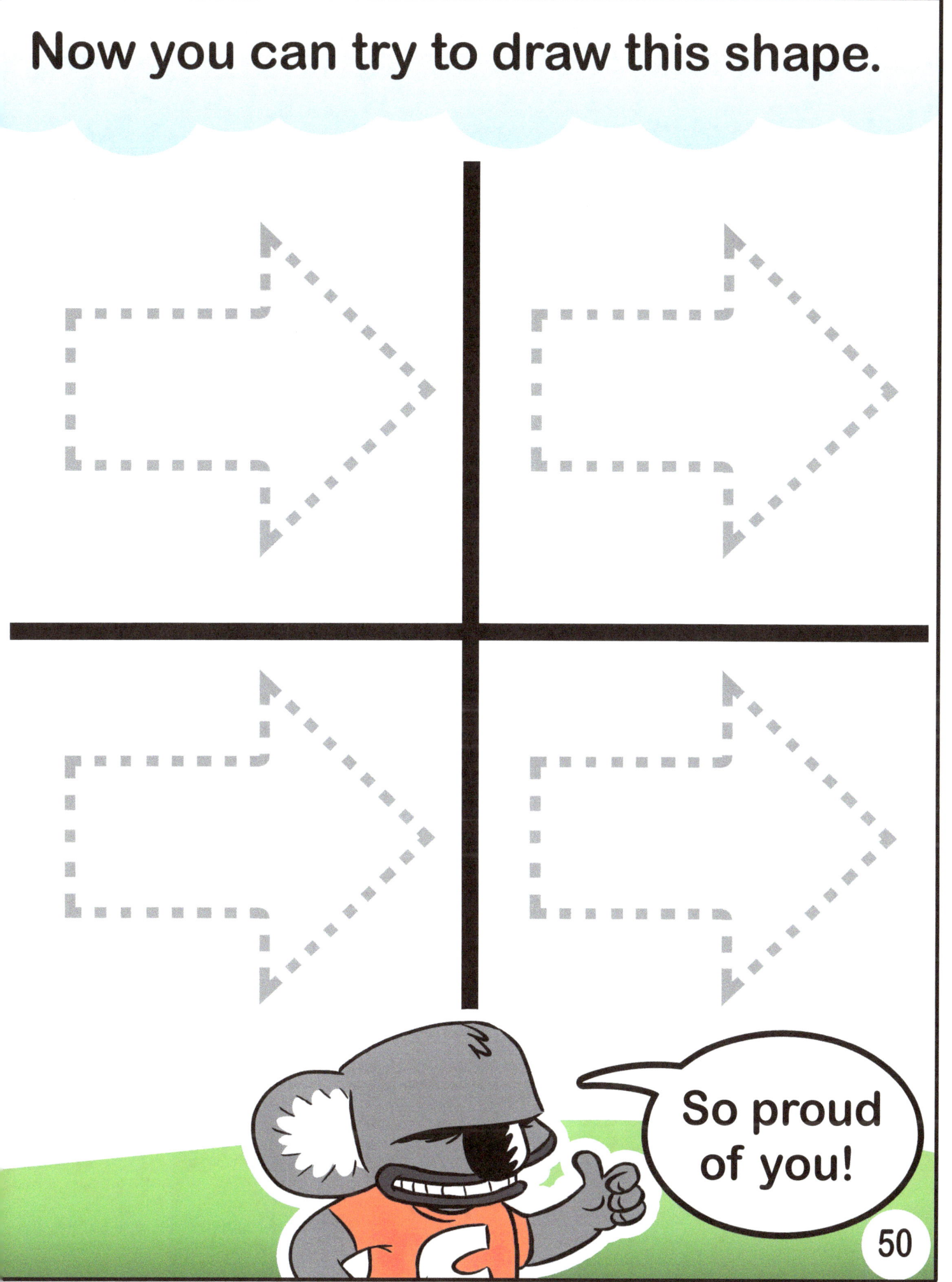

So proud of you!

www.ingramcontent.com/pod-product-compliance
Lightning Source LLC
Chambersburg PA
CBHW081305170526
45165CB00011B/3416